Grand Diplôme® Cooking Course

Volume 11

Grand Diplôme® Cooking Course

A Danbury Press Book

The Danbury Press

a division of Grolier Enterprises, Inc.

Robert B. Clarke   Publisher

This book has been adapted from the Grand Diplôme Cooking Course, originally published by Purnell Cookery, U.S.A.

Purnell Grand Diplôme Editorial Board

Rosemary Hume and Muriel Downes
Principals, London Cordon Bleu Cookery
School, England

Anne Willan	Editor
Eleanor Noderer	Associate Editor
Sheryl Julian	Assistant Editor
John Paton	Managing Editor
José Northey	Co-ordinating Editor
Peter Leather	Art Editor
Charles F. Turgeon	Wine Consultant
Joy Langridge	Consultant Editor

Library of Congress Catalog Card Number: 72-13896
© Phoebus Publishing Company/BPC Publishing Limited, 1971/1972/1979
Filmsetting by Petty and Sons Ltd., Leeds, England.
Printed in the United States of America

4567899

All recipes have been tested either at the Cordon Bleu Cookery School in London or in our U.S. test kitchens.

Note: all recipe quantities in this book serve 4 people unless otherwise stated.

Contents

From the Editor

The robust aroma of hot beer soup, spicy sausages, roast venison, sauerbraten and red cabbage epitomizes the appeal of **German Cooking**. Continue your travels with Volume 11 of your Grand Diplome Cooking Course and sample some of the many **Tropical Dishes** from South America, the Caribbean, Australasia, Southeast Asia and Africa. You will find such exotic recipes as calalou, a zesty crab stew with okra and greens from the Caribbean or feijoada, the meat, sausage and bean stew that is the national dish of Brazil.

Return home to solve the problems of **Cooking For Two** with menus (devised by the Cordon Bleu Cookery School of London) centered on spiced chicken, Mexican style, or a delicious veal goulash, enriched with sour cream. Become an expert on the methods of preparing the many types of **Fish** that abound in American waters or, if you are a meat lover, try one of the **Unusual Meat Dishes** like moussaka, made with lamb, eggplant and potatoes topped with béchamel sauce and cheese.

Two traditional skills are brought up to date in the lessons on **Preserves** and how to make **Ice Cream**. Satin smooth, riotously rich, homemade ice cream is as rare these days as an old-fashioned ice cream parlor with wrought-iron chairs. If you can't buy fresh ice cream around the corner, why not try preparing your own special brand at home — caramel pecan, pistachio or a colorful strawberry sherbet. Then carry summer into winter with the many fruits of fall and produce your own crystal clear jellies, creamy fruit butters, jams, pickles and chutneys.

In our **Menus** you will find ideas for elegant and informal entertaining, with timetables to make preparation easy. So to you and your guests — Bon Appétit!

Anne Willan

Some of the dishes for a simple buffet supper are, from left to right: onion quiche and bread rolls, les crudités (a fresh vegetable salad) and a wassail bowl; tomato flan and a bowl of apples

WELCOME THE WINTER WITH A BUFFET

Offer a warm welcome with a casual buffet table. Tempt appetites with Scotch eggs or a fish pâté, bake a choice of hot and cold savory pies and serve them with relishes, a fresh vegetable salad and spicy chicken legs with deviled crackers. Dessert couldn't be simpler — a homemade orange gelatin laden with fresh fruit, and a cake traditionally served on Twelfth Night.

To set the festive mood, serve an old English wassail bowl of hot cider with oranges and lemons, or offer steaming mugs of lambs' wool — ale enriched with baked apple and spiced with cinnamon. The recipes, served together, are enough for 16 people.

Scotch Eggs
Kipper Pâté & Deviled Crackers

Deviled Chicken
Les Crudités (Fresh Vegetable Salad)
Beef Flan   Onion Quiche
or
Leek & Bacon Pie   Tomato Flan
Assorted Relishes

Fresh Fruit Gelatin
Twelfth Night Cake

Wassail Bowl   Lambs' Wool

TIMETABLE

3–4 weeks before
Make Twelfth Night cake and store in airtight container. (The earlier the cake is made, the better the flavor.)

Day before
Hard cook eggs for Scotch eggs.
Poach kippers and make pâté. Store, covered, in refrigerator.
Make dressing for les crudités.
Make pastry dough for the quiche, flans and pie and chill. Line flan rings or pie pans, wrap in plastic bags and refrigerate.
Prepare all relishes and keep covered in bowls in the refrigerator.
Prepare devil mixture for chicken.
Simmer chicken, cool, drain and remove skin; cover and refrigerate.

Morning
Make coating for Scotch eggs, coat eggs and deep fry; cool and cover but do not refrigerate unless kitchen is very hot.
Prepare vegetables for les crudités; keep covered in refrigerator. Do not add dressing.
Make fresh fruit gelatin and leave covered in refrigerator.
Bake beef flan shell blind. Make the filling and put in the pastry shell. Make potato garnish, pipe on top, cover and refrigerate *or prepare filling for tomato flan, fill flan shell, bake and cool; keep covered in refrigerator.*

Prepare filling for onion quiche, bake and cool; cover and refrigerate *or prepare filling for leek and bacon pie, bake and cool; keep covered in refrigerator.*
Prepare ingredients for wassail bowl or lambs' wool but do not heat.

Before serving
Arrange pâté in a bowl.
Make deviled crackers.
Add dressing to les crudités and arrange on platter.
Let fresh fruit gelatin come to room temperature before serving. Whip cream for serving and chill.
Take out all relishes for serving.
Bake beef flan in a hot oven (425°F) for 15 minutes or until lightly browned, *or reheat tomato flan if serving hot in moderate oven (350°F) for 10–15 minutes.*
Reheat onion quiche *or leek and bacon pie* if serving hot in moderate oven (350°F) for 10–15 minutes.
Set Twelfth Night cake on a platter.
Broil chicken with devil sauce; arrange on a platter.
Heat the rolls.
Heat prepared drinks, pour into bowls or glasses and serve.

> You will find that **cooking times** given in the individual recipes for these dishes have sometimes been adapted in the timetable to help you when cooking and serving this menu as a party meal.

Scotch Eggs

8 hard-cooked eggs
1 lb pork sausage meat
1 teaspoon chopped mixed herbs (sage, thyme, marjoram)
salt and pepper

For coating
$\frac{1}{2}$ cup seasoned flour (made with $\frac{1}{2}$ teaspoon salt, $\frac{1}{4}$ teaspoon pepper)
1 egg, beaten to mix
1 cup dry white breadcrumbs
deep fat (for frying)

Serves 8 people.

Method
Peel the eggs and put them into cold water. Mix the sausage meat with the herbs and seasoning. Dry the eggs thoroughly.
Divide the sausage meat into 8 equal portions and pat each portion into a round on a dampened board. Surround each egg completely with the sausage meat, then roll in the seasoned flour, brush with beaten egg and coat well with the crumbs.
Fry the Scotch eggs in hot deep fat (375°F on a fat thermometer) until they are a rich brown. Remove from the fat and drain on paper towels. Cool the eggs before cutting in half to serve cold.

Pat out equal portions of the seasoned sausage meat; mold around the hard-cooked eggs

Fry the coated Scotch eggs in hot deep fat until they are a rich brown

> **Note:** the recipes in this menu, served together, are enough for 16 people.

Scotch eggs — hard-cooked eggs wrapped in sausage meat and deep fried — are cooled and halved to serve

Kipper Pâté

3–4 kippers
1 package (8 oz) cream cheese
$\frac{1}{4}$ teaspoon paprika
black pepper, freshly ground
1–2 tablespoons light cream
salt (optional)

Serves 8 people.

Method
Poach kippers in water to cover for 5–6 minutes, cool them slightly in the liquid and remove skin and bones; there should be about $1\frac{1}{2}$ cups fish.

Work the cheese until it is smooth and creamy and add paprika and pepper. Stir in the cream.

Pound the fish in a mortar and pestle until smooth and work into the cheese mixture or purée the mixture in the blender or beat well with an electric mixer until the pâté is soft and light. Taste for seasoning, spoon it into a bowl and serve with deviled crackers.

Deviled Crackers

Brush matzo or unsalted crackers with melted butter, sprinkle with cayenne and heat in a hot oven (400°F) for 5 minutes or until very hot.

Deviled Chicken

16 chicken legs
2 onions, sliced
2 carrots, sliced
bouquet garni
10 peppercorns
salt
bunch of watercress (for garnish) – optional

For devil mixture
$\frac{3}{4}$ cup butter
3 tablespoons ketchup
3 tablespoons Worcestershire sauce
1$\frac{1}{2}$ teaspoons ground mace
3 tablespoons chutney
1 teaspoon anchovy paste
white pepper
$\frac{1}{4}$ teaspoon cayenne or dash of Tabasco (optional)

This recipe can be made with chicken legs only or with legs and thighs. Serves 6–8 people.

Method
Put the chicken pieces into a large pan with the sliced vegetables, bouquet garni, peppercorns, a little salt and water barely to cover. Cover pan and cook over low heat for about 15 minutes. Cool the chicken pieces slightly in the liquid.

To prepare devil mixture: cream the butter thoroughly and gradually mix in the rest of the ingredients with salt and pepper. Season the sauce with cayenne or a dash of Tabasco to make it hot if you like.

Remove the partly cooked chicken pieces from the liquid and pat them dry with paper towels. Strip off the skin, slash meat with the point of a knife and rub a little of the devil mixture on each piece.

Place the chicken pieces in a broiling pan and broil for 6 minutes or until well browned. Turn the pieces once during broiling and baste with the remaining devil mixture and any pan drippings.

Let the pieces cool slightly and pile them on a platter. Garnish with watercress, if you like.

Les Crudités
(Fresh Vegetable Salad)

4 carrots
4 medium cooked beets
4–6 medium white turnips
1 small head of green cabbage
small bunch of celery
1 cup vinaigrette dressing
bunch of watercress (for garnish)

Add dressing to this salad not more than 1 hour before serving. Serves 16 people.

Method
Grate the carrots, beets and turnips separately on a very fine grater and put each in a separate bowl. Shred the cabbage, cut the celery into sticks and put them in separate bowls. Moisten each vegetable with a little vinaigrette dressing and arrange each one in sections in a large salad bowl or on a platter.

Arrange a bunch of watercress in the center and serve the salad with hot rolls.

Note: the recipes in this menu, served together, are enough for 16 people.

Beef Flan

2 cup quantity of rich pie pastry (see right)

For filling
1$\frac{1}{2}$ lb lean ground beef
1–2 tablespoons oil
2 onions, finely chopped
2 tablespoons flour
1–1$\frac{1}{2}$ cups stock or water
salt and pepper
Worcestershire sauce (to taste)

For topping
4 medium potatoes
2–3 tablespoons butter
$\frac{1}{2}$ cup hot milk
2 egg yolks (optional)

10 inch flan ring or pie pan; pastry bag and large star tube

Serves 6 people.

Method
Prepare the pastry dough and chill 30 minutes. Roll out and line the flan ring or pie pans. Prick the pastry bottom with a fork and chill 15 minutes.

Set oven at hot (400°F).

Bake the flan shell blind in the heated oven for 20–25 minutes or until lightly browned; let cool.

To make the filling: heat the oil in a skillet or flame-proof casserole, add the onion and cook until soft. Add beef and cook, stirring, for 2–3 minutes or until brown. Take from heat, stir in flour and pour in the stock or water. Season and continue to cook, stirring, until the mixture boils.

Cover and cook $\frac{3}{4}$–1 hour over low heat, stirring occasionally, until the mixture is thick and creamy; if necessary add a little more liquid as the beef cooks. Stir in Worcestershire sauce and seasoning to taste.

Set oven at hot (425°F).

To make the topping: boil potatoes for 15–20 minutes until tender; drain thoroughly and mash or work through a sieve. Add butter and hot milk and beat until smooth but firm; beat in egg yolks, if used.

Fill flan shell with beef mixture; put potato mixture into the pastry bag fitted with a star tube. Pipe potato mixture around the edge and across the pie in a lattice pattern. Bake flan in heated oven for 15 minutes or until lightly browned. Serve hot.

Rich Pie Pastry

For 2 cup quantity: sift 2 cups flour with a pinch of salt into a bowl. Cut $\frac{1}{2}$ cup butter and 2 tablespoons shortening into the flour until in small pieces and coated. Rub in with the fingertips until the mixture resembles crumbs.

Make a well in the center, add 1 egg yolk, 3 tablespoons water and stir to combine. Draw the flour into the center quickly with a knife, adding more water if necessary, to form a smooth dough.

Turn the dough onto a floured board or marble slab and knead lightly until smooth. Wrap it in wax paper and chill 30 minutes.

Party dishes are: kipper pâté with deviled crackers, beef flan in center with accompanying relishes, and at back, fresh fruit gelatin

Onion Quiche

2 cup quantity of rich pie pastry
(see page 12)

For filling
4 large onions, finely sliced
$\frac{1}{4}$ cup butter
6–8 slices of bacon, diced
3 eggs
salt and pepper
$\frac{1}{2}$ cup milk
$\frac{1}{2}$ cup light cream
2–3 tablespoons Parmesan
  cheese
1 tablespoon melted butter

10 inch flan ring or pie pan

Serves 6 people.

Method
Prepare the pastry dough and
chill 30 minutes. Roll out and
line the flan ring or pie pan.
Prick the pastry bottom with a
fork and chill.

Set oven at hot (400°F).

To make the filling: blanch
the onions, drain them well,
then cook gently in the pan
with the butter until golden
and tender. Remove them,
fry the diced bacon in the
same pan until crisp, drain
and add the bacon to the
onions.

Beat the eggs with a fork
until mixed and stir in the
seasoning, milk, cream and
onion mixture. Pour the filling
into the pastry shell and
sprinkle with Parmesan cheese
and the melted butter.

Bake the quiche in the
heated oven for 10–12 minutes to set the pastry, then
lower the heat to moderately
hot (375°F) and bake 20
minutes longer or until the
filling is golden brown and set.
Serve hot or cold.

Alternative entrées

Leek and Bacon Pie

$1\frac{1}{2}$ cup quantity puff pastry
(see Volume 8)
1 egg, beaten to mix with
  $\frac{1}{2}$ teaspoon salt (for glaze)

For filling
10 leeks
$\frac{1}{2}$ lb sliced bacon
3 eggs
salt and pepper
4–5 tablespoons light cream
1 cup chicken or veal stock

9 inch flan ring or deep pie pan

Serves 6 people.

Method
To prepare the filling: trim and
discard the roots and green
tops from the leeks; split them
lengthwise, wash well and cut
into diagonal slices, about 1
inch wide. Put the slices into
a pan of boiling salted water
and simmer 4–5 minutes or
until tender. Drain well.

Cut the bacon into $\frac{1}{2}$ inch
strips, put into a pan of cold
water and bring to a boil;
drain.

Break the eggs into a bowl,
beat with a fork, season and
stir in the cream. Add the
leeks, bacon and stock.

Set oven at hot (400°F).

Roll out two-thirds of the
dough thinly and line the flan
ring or pie pan, overlapping
the edge slightly. Prick the
bottom with a fork and pour in
leek mixture. Roll out remain-
ing dough about $\frac{1}{4}$ inch thick,
place it on top of pie, press
down around edges and trim.

Mark the top of the dough
in a lattice pattern with the
back of a knife and make a
hole in the top to let steam
escape. Roll out the pastry
trimmings and cut into leaves,
flowers or other decorations
and place them around hole.

Scallop the edge of the pie
with your fingers, brush the
top with egg glaze and chill
15–30 minutes.

Before baking, put a baking
sheet into the oven for several
minutes to heat thoroughly.
Then set the flan ring (on a
baking sheet) or pie pan on the
pre-heated baking sheet so
the bottom of the pie will be
well cooked from the addi-
tional heat. Bake in heated
oven 25–30 minutes or until
the pastry is golden brown
and a skewer inserted in the
center of the pie comes out
clean. Serve hot or cold.

To make a Pastry Rose
Roll out piece of pastry dough
thinly, about 4 inches square,
and sprinkle with flour. Fold in
half, sprinkle it with flour
and fold over again, making a
2-inch square.

Shape the pastry dough
into a ball over your thumb.
Remove it, cut a cross through
the top layer of pastry, fold
back 4 petals and repeat this
twice more to leave one uncut
layer.

Tomato Flan

2 cup quantity of rich pie pastry
(see box on page 12)

For filling
6 tomatoes, peeled, halved and
  seeded
salt and pepper
$1\frac{1}{2}$ cups browned breadcrumbs
2 cups grated Gruyère or
  Cheddar cheese
$\frac{3}{4}$ cup heavy cream
1 tablespoon chopped mixed
  herbs (parsley, chives,
  oregano)
1 tablespoon anchovy paste
pinch of nutmeg (optional)

10 inch flan ring or pie pan

Serves 6 people.

Method
Make the pastry dough; chill
30 minutes. Roll out and line
the flan ring or pan. Prick the
pastry bottom with a fork;
chill. Set oven at hot (400°F).

To make the filling: sprinkle
the tomatoes with salt and let
stand about 30 minutes. Drain
off all liquid and pat dry with
paper towels.

Sprinkle breadcrumbs over
the bottom of the flan shell
and arrange tomatoes on
top in a single layer, rounded
sides up.

Combine the cheese, cream,
herbs and anchovy paste and
season well, adding a pinch of
nutmeg, if you like. Spoon
over the tomatoes and bake
the flan in heated oven for
30–40 minutes.

If the flan browns too
quickly, lower heat to moderate (350°F) after 25 minutes
and continue baking until the
pastry shrinks slightly from
the sides of the flan ring or
pie pan. Serve hot or cold.

Accompanying Relishes

Spiced Cucumber Relish

3 cucumbers, peeled, seeded
   and diced
salt
3-inch stick of cinnamon
½ teaspoon mustard seed
6 whole cloves
1 cup distilled white vinegar
½ cup sugar
1 teaspoon turmeric
2 medium onions, chopped

Serves 6 people.

Method
Sprinkle the cucumber with salt; let stand 30 minutes and rinse.

Tie the cinnamon, mustard seed and cloves in a cheesecloth bag and add to vinegar with sugar and turmeric. Heat until the sugar dissolves, then simmer 5 minutes.

Add the cucumber and onion and cook gently for 15–20 minutes or until tender and yellow from the turmeric. Remove the cheesecloth bag and cool. Pile the relish into a serving dish and chill.

Note: the recipes in this menu, served together, are enough for 16 people.

Onion Relish

4 Bermuda or other mild
   onions, sliced and blanched
2 cups (½ lb) mushrooms,
   thickly sliced
¼ cup water
juice of ½ lemon
salt and pepper
½ cup vinaigrette dressing
2 tablespoons chopped parsley
   (optional)

Serves 6 people.

Method
Push the blanched onion slices into rings, cover with cold water and simmer until barely tender. Drain.

Cook mushrooms in the water with the lemon juice and seasoning for 1 minute or until soft. Drain thoroughly. Mix them with the onion, moisten with vinaigrette dressing and pile into a serving dish. Sprinkle with chopped parsley, if you like, before serving.

Beet Relish

2 cups finely chopped cooked
   or canned beets, drained
3 tart apples, pared, cored and
   diced
½ cup vinaigrette dressing
   (with a little crushed garlic
   added)

Serves 6 people.

Method
Combine the beets and apples and moisten with vinaigrette dressing. Toss the relish, pile into a serving dish and chill.

Celery and Cheese Relish

4 stalks of celery
½ lb Gouda or mild Cheddar
   cheese, diced
3–4 green peppers, cored,
   seeded, chopped and
   blanched
½ cup vinaigrette dressing

Serves 6 people.

Method
Soak the celery in ice water for 1 hour to make it crisp. Chop it coarsely and mix with the green peppers. Add the diced cheese and moisten with vinaigrette dressing. Pile into a serving dish and chill.

Tomato and Anchovy Relish

6 ripe tomatoes, peeled,
   seeded and cut in strips
1 tablespoon anchovy paste
2 tablespoons vinegar
6 tablespoons oil
2 tablespoons heavy cream
black pepper, freshly ground

Serves 6 people.

Method
Beat together all the ingredients except the tomatoes to make a dressing; season well with pepper. Spoon the dressing over the tomatoes, toss gently, pile them into a serving dish and chill.

Italian Relish

6 tomatoes, peeled, seeded and
   finely chopped
4 onions, chopped
4 slices of canned pimiento,
   drained and chopped
4 pickled green tomatoes,
   drained and chopped
3 tablespoons olive oil
1 tablespoon white vinegar
1½ teaspoons oregano
1½ teaspoons salt
pepper, freshly ground

Serves 6 people.

Method
Mix all the vegetables with olive oil, vinegar, oregano, salt and a little pepper. Pile the relish into a serving dish, cover and chill.

A steaming mug of spiced lambs' wool accompanies Twelfth Night cake

Fresh Fruit Gelatin

6 tangerines
4 ripe dessert pears
1 lb black or seedless green
  grapes
5 envelopes gelatin
1½ quarts water
3 cups sugar
peeled rind and juice of
  3 lemons
2 cans (12 oz each) frozen
  concentrated orange juice,
  diluted with 1 quart cold
  water
1½ cups heavy cream, stiffly
  whipped (to serve)

Glass bowl (4 quart capacity)

Serves 16 people.

Method
Sprinkle the gelatin over 1½ cups of the water in a bowl and let stand 5 minutes or until spongy.

Heat the sugar with the remaining water, lemon rind and juice until sugar has dissolved and simmer 5 minutes. Strain and, while very hot, stir in the softened gelatin until it dissolves. Stir in the diluted orange juice and let cool.

Peel and section the tangerines; pare, core and slice the pears; remove the seeds from the grapes, if necessary.

Put the fruit in the glass bowl and pour in the cooled gelatin. Cover and chill in the refrigerator until set. Serve a bowl of whipped cream separately.

Note: the recipes in this menu, served together, are enough for 16 people.

Twelfth Night Cake

1 cup butter
¾ cup sugar
3 eggs
3 cups flour
1 teaspoon ground cinnamon
¼ teaspoon ground allspice
¼ teaspoon ground cloves
½ teaspoon salt
¾ cup currants
¾ cup golden raisins
¼ cup chopped candied citron
  peel
¼ cup chopped candied
  orange peel
¼ cup slivered almonds
¼ cup milk

For topping
3–4 tablespoons apricot jam
  glaze
¼ cup finely chopped candied
  citron peel
¼ cup finely chopped candied
  lemon peel
½ cup candied cherries

10 inch tube pan

Method
Grease cake pan and line it with wax paper; set oven at low (300°F).

Cream the butter, gradually add the sugar and beat until the mixture is soft and light. Add the eggs, one at a time, and beat thoroughly after each addition.

Sift the flour with the spices and salt and divide it into 3 portions.

Mix 1 portion with the candied fruits and nuts so they are well coated. Stir 1 portion of the flour into the egg mixture with half the milk, then stir in the fruit and nut mixture, then the remaining portion of flour and milk.

Transfer the cake batter to the prepared cake pan, smooth the top and bake in heated oven 1½–1¾ hours or until a skewer inserted in the center comes out clean. If the cake gets very brown before the end of cooking, cover with a sheet of foil. Cool the cake for 30 minutes in the pan, then turn out and cool completely on a wire rack.

To decorate, brush the top of the cake with apricot jam glaze and sprinkle chopped citron and lemon peel on top. Arrange candied cherries around the edge and in the center, if you like.

Wassail Bowl

4 quarts cider
3 oranges
3 lemons
2–3 sticks of cinnamon
1 tablespoon allspice
1½ quarts water
1½ cups sugar
1 lemon, sliced (for garnish)

Traditionally this recipe is made with hard cider, so for an alcoholic drink, substitute 4 quarts hard cider for the regular cider.

Serves 18–20 people.

Method
Peel the rind from the oranges and lemons and put rind in a pan with the spices and water. Cover and simmer 2½ hours.

Squeeze the juice from the oranges and lemons and strain it.

Strain the hot liquid over the sugar and add the fruit juices and cider. Heat almost to boiling, but do not boil. Serve very hot with the sliced lemon floating on top.

Lambs' Wool

4 quarts ale
4½ cups sweet white wine
1 teaspoon grated nutmeg
1 teaspoon ground ginger
1 stick of cinnamon
4–5 baked apples
  (see Volume 5)
brown sugar (to taste)
20–24 extra sticks of cinnamon
  (for serving)

Serves 20–24 people.

Method
Heat the ale, wine and spices together in a large pan but do not boil. Pare the baked apples, removing the cores, and mash the flesh to a pulp with a fork.

Stir the apple purée into the liquid, remove the cinnamon stick and mix together well. Work the mixture through a strainer, pressing it thoroughly. Add the brown sugar to taste and serve hot with a cinnamon stick in each mug.

In England during Tudor times the sheep shearing season was ushered in with 'lamb' ale and much feasting. The shepherd whose flock had produced the earliest lamb was elected shepherd king.

The word **wassail** comes from the old English 'waes hal' meaning 'be well'. It was the traditional toast given in medieval times when drinking Christmas spiced ale or wine.

Make an unusual casserole for two with lamb chops, sliced eggplant, tomatoes and cheese

COOKING FOR TWO

It's easy to broil a steak or toss a salad, but to serve original, appetizing menus for two, day after day, requires careful planning. Look for ingredients that come in small quantities — pieces of chicken, chicken livers, fish fillets, chops, variety meats — most are excellent buys. Some, like scallops and steak, are expensive but will vary your menus.

Quick dishes are ideal but these also tend to be expensive because only the best cuts of meat can be cooked in a short time. However, stews and pot roasts reheat well, so make enough for four, refrigerate and serve the leftovers a few days later. (Be sure to reheat food thoroughly and quickly when using leftovers.) Most roasting cuts are very large for two people, but you can slice the meat for cold cuts and add a homemade relish, or dice the meat and reheat it in a curry sauce.

Bake leftover fish, ham and vegetables in a quiche or savory pie or add them to cooked rice with butter, cream and parsley to make a risotto.

Lamb Chops with Eggplant

4 lamb chops
1 medium eggplant, sliced
2 tablespoons oil
2 tablespoons butter
2 onions, sliced
1 clove of garlic, crushed
1 teaspoon tomato paste
$\frac{1}{2}$ cup stock
2–3 tomatoes, peeled, seeded and sliced
salt and pepper
2 tablespoons grated Parmesan or Cheddar cheese
1 tablespoon chopped parsley

Method

Score the eggplant slices with a knife and sprinkle with a little salt; let stand 30 minutes to draw out the juices (dégorger). Drain and rinse them with cold water and drain again. Dry eggplant slices with paper towels.

Heat the oil and butter in a frying pan and brown the chops quickly on both sides. Remove them, lower the heat slightly and brown the onions. Take them out, add the eggplant and fry over medium heat for 2–3 minutes on each side or until brown, adding more oil if necessary.

Replace the onions, add the garlic, tomato paste, stock, tomatoes and season; bring the mixture to a boil. Spoon half the mixture into a casserole (or a flameproof one if cooking on top of the stove),

place the chops on top and cover with the rest of the eggplant and tomato mixture.

Sprinkle the top with grated cheese and bake, uncovered, in a moderate oven (350°F) or simmer, covered, on top of the stove for 35–40 minutes. Sprinkle the top with parsley before serving.

Quality of Lamb Chops

Cost of chops is directly proportional to their quality. **Loin** and **rib chops** are the best as the meat is sweet and delicate and, when properly trimmed, they include very little fat.

Sirloin chops have a larger ratio of meat to bone than loin chops but the flavor is less delicate. **Arm** and **blade chops,** cut from the shoulder, are the least expensive; the flavor is good but they contain a fair amount of bone and tough connective tissue.

Occasionally it is possible to buy **leg chops** or steaks, although most markets prefer to sell the leg whole for roasting. Leg chops are juicy and lean but they must be cooked carefully or they will dry and toughen.

Apple Custard

1 large dessert apple, pared, cored and chopped
1 egg
1 egg yolk
1 cup milk
1 tablespoon honey

2 custard cups or individual baking dishes

Method

Butter the custard cups or baking dishes and pile the chopped apple in the bottom.

Beat the egg and egg yolk until thoroughly mixed. Heat the milk with the honey until the honey is dissolved and stir into the egg mixture. When thoroughly blended, strain onto the apples and set the cups in a water bath.

Bake in a moderate oven (350°F) for 20 minutes or until a knife inserted in the custard comes out clean. Serve hot or cold.

Peach, Cherry or Strawberry Custard

Make as for apple custard above, using 1–2 chopped peaches, or 1 cup of chopped cherries or strawberries.

Kidney Potatoes

4 baking potatoes
salt
1 tablespoon chopped parsley (for sprinkling)

For filling
2 lamb's kidneys
4 slices of bacon
$\frac{1}{2}$ teaspoon prepared mustard
pepper, freshly ground
2 shallots or scallions, finely chopped
1 teaspoon mixed chopped chives and thyme
2 teaspoons chopped parsley

Method

Set oven at moderate (350°F).

Scrub the potatoes, roll them lightly in salt, prick and bake in heated oven for $1-1\frac{1}{4}$ hours or until they yield when pressed.

To make filling: remove skin from kidneys, halve them and cut out core with scissors. Flatten the bacon, spread it with mustard and sprinkle with pepper, shallots or scallions and herbs. Place one half kidney on each slice of bacon and roll up.

Cut the top lengthwise from the cooked potatoes, scoop out enough of the pulp to make room for the kidneys, put inside and cover with a little of the scooped out pulp. Replace the lid, if you like, or roughen potato pulp with a fork. Bake in the oven 30–35 minutes longer or until the bacon is cooked bu the kidney is still rare in the center. Sprinkle with parsley before serving.

Put kidney, wrapped in bacon, into the hollowed-out baked potato before final baking

Baked potatoes are stuffed with kidneys and bacon, then browned in the oven

Eggplant Casserole

1 medium eggplant, sliced
salt
$\frac{1}{4}$ cup oil
$\frac{1}{2}$ cup tomato sauce
1 cup yogurt
black pepper, freshly ground

Method

Score the eggplant slices with a knife, sprinkle them lightly with salt and let stand 30 minutes to draw out the juices (dégorger). Drain and rinse them with cold water. Drain again.

Set oven at moderate (350°F).

Dry the eggplant slices with paper towels. Heat the oil in a skillet and fry the eggplant a few slices at a time for 2–3 minutes or until golden on both sides.

Lay the slices in a baking dish in layers with the tomato sauce, yogurt and black pepper, finishing with a layer of eggplant. Cover and bake in heated oven for about 40 minutes. Turn out the eggplant onto a platter to serve.

Chocolate and Macaroon Mousse

3 squares (3 oz) sweet chocolate, chopped
2 large macaroons
1 tablespoon brandy
2 tablespoons strong black coffee
2 eggs, separated
1 tablespoon unsalted butter
$\frac{1}{4}$ cup heavy cream, stiffly whipped (for decoration) – optional

2 mousse pots or custard cups; pastry bag and star tube (optional)

Method

Set the oven at moderately hot (325°F).

Break the macaroons into small pieces, spread them in a pan or on a baking sheet and bake in the heated oven for 5–10 minutes or until they are golden and crisp. Cool them and crush with a rolling pin. Divide the crumbs evenly between the mousse pots, spoon over the brandy and let soak.

Put the chocolate in a small saucepan with the coffee and melt it very slowly over a bowl of hot water, stirring occasionally. Beat in the egg yolks, one by one, and then the butter, a small piece at a time. Cool to lukewarm.

Whisk the egg whites until they hold a stiff peak and fold into the chocolate mixture. Pour it into the mousse pots and let set.

Serve the mousse plain or, if you like, put the whipped cream into a pastry bag fitted with a star tube and pipe a rosette on top of each mousse.

Note: all quantities given here are for 2 servings only.

Menu 3

Quick Consommé
Halibut with Shrimp Sauce
Brazilian Bananas

Quick Consommé

For hot consommé: heat 1 can consommé and, just before serving, add 1 tablespoon brandy or sherry and 1 tomato, peeled, seeded and cut in strips.

For jellied consommé: stir 1 tablespoon sherry or brandy into 1 can consommé and chill until set. Stir lightly to break up the consommé and pile in bowls. Top with a tablespoon of sour cream and a little red or black caviar or a few chopped chives.

Halibut with Shrimp Sauce

$\frac{3}{4}$–1 lb halibut steaks
juice of $\frac{1}{2}$ lemon
salt
$\frac{1}{2}$ cup water

For shrimp sauce
$\frac{1}{2}$ cup ($\frac{1}{4}$ lb) peeled, cooked baby shrimps
2 tablespoons butter
2 tablespoons flour
$1\frac{1}{2}$ cups milk (infused with slice of onion, 6 peppercorns, $\frac{1}{2}$ bay leaf and blade of mace)
pepper
2 tablespoons heavy cream (optional)

Method

Wash the fish steaks and pat dry with paper towels. Lay them in a buttered baking dish, sprinkle with lemon juice and a little salt and pour over the water. Cover with foil and poach in a moderate oven (350°F) for 15–20 minutes or until the fish flakes easily when tested with a fork.

To make the shrimp sauce: melt the butter, stir in flour off the heat and pour in the infused milk. Bring to a boil, stirring, and cook 2 minutes. Take from the heat, add the shrimps with seasoning to taste and reheat without boiling. Stir in the cream if used.

Drain the fish steaks and transfer them to a platter. Serve the sauce separately.

Brazilian Bananas

3 bananas
1 tablespoon rum
2 teaspoons dry instant coffee
2 teaspoons sugar
$\frac{1}{2}$ cup heavy cream, whipped until it holds a stiff peak
2 tablespoons shredded almonds, browned

Method

Peel the bananas and slice them thickly into a serving bowl or sherbet glasses and sprinkle over the rum. Dissolve the coffee in 1–2 tablespoons boiling water, add the sugar and cool.

Add the coffee mixture to the whipped cream and whip again until stiff. Cover the bananas with the coffee-flavored cream, sprinkle with shredded almonds and serve chilled.

Brazilian bananas are topped with coffee-flavored whipped cream

Serve veal goulash with buttered noodles

Menu 4

Veal Goulash
Buttered Noodles
or Boulangère Potatoes
Lemon Pie

Veal Goulash

1 lb shoulder or round of veal,
  cut in large cubes
2 tablespoons oil
1 large onion, finely sliced
2 teaspoons paprika
2 teaspoons flour
1 small clove of garlic, crushed
  (optional)
2 teaspoons tomato paste
1½ cups stock or water
1 bay leaf
1 tomato, peeled, seeded and
  cut in strips
salt and pepper
½ cup yogurt
1 tablespoon chopped parsley

Method

In a flameproof casserole heat the oil and brown the meat a few pieces at a time on all sides over medium heat. Take out, add the onion and cook until very soft.

Stir in the paprika and cook, stirring, over low heat for 1 minute. Stir in the flour, garlic, if used, tomato paste, stock or water and bay leaf and bring slowly to a boil.

Put back the meat, add seasoning, cover and bake in a moderate oven (350°F) or simmer on top of the stove for 1¼–1½ hours or until the veal is very tender.

Add the tomato 10 minutes before the end of cooking. Remove the bay leaf, adjust the seasoning and spoon over the yogurt. Sprinkle with parsley before serving.

If you cook the goulash on top of the stove, serve it with buttered noodles or, when cooking in the oven, bake a dish of boulangère potatoes at the same time.

Buttered Noodles

½ lb noodles
2 tablespoons butter
salt
black pepper, freshly ground

Method

Cook the noodles in plenty of boiling salted water, 2–3 quarts at least, for 8–10 minutes. Stir gently from time to time to prevent the noodles from sticking to the bottom of the pan. When cooked, they should look creamy and opaque and can be severed with a thumbnail (or taste one to see if done).

Watchpoint: do not over-cook the noodles as they become sticky and pasty.

Pour the noodles at once into a colander, rinse in hot water and drain well. Rinse the pan used to cook the noodles and add the butter. Return the noodles to the pan and toss over low heat for 1–2 minutes. Season with salt and black pepper.

If the noodles must be kept hot before serving, pour about 1 cup hot water into the pan, put in the drained noodles, cover and keep warm at the side of the stove. When ready to serve, drain off the water, add butter and seasonings and toss.

Boulangère Potatoes

¾–1 lb potatoes
2–3 medium onions, sliced
salt and pepper
1 bay leaf
1 cup stock
1 tablespoon drippings
  or butter

Method

First blanch the onions. Put them in cold water, bring to a boil and boil 1 minute before draining. Peel and slice the potatoes thinly and arrange at once in layers with the onions in a shallow ovenproof dish, seasoning each layer with salt and pepper.

Add the bay leaf with enough stock to cover the potatoes, dot with drippings or butter and bake in a moderate oven (350°F) for 1 hour or until the potatoes are soft and well browned.

Halfway through cooking if the top layer of potatoes has curled, press it down into the stock with a spoon and add a little more drippings. If necessary, add more stock – the potatoes should be soft and moist when cooked, but not wet.

Lemon Pie

For graham cracker crust
⅔ cup graham cracker crumbs
1 tablespoon sugar
2 tablespoons melted butter

For filling
6 tablespoons fresh lemon juice
2 eggs, separated
1 can (8 oz) condensed milk
⅓ cup sugar
½ teaspoon vanilla

6 inch pie pan

Method

Set the oven at moderately low (325°F).

To make the pie shell: mix the cracker crumbs, sugar and melted butter together thoroughly and press into the sides and base of the pie pan.

To make the filling: beat the egg yolks until light and beat in the condensed milk and lemon juice until the mixture is thick. Pour into the pie shell.

Beat the egg whites until they hold a stiff peak. Beat in 4 teaspoons sugar until the mixture is glossy, and then fold in the remaining sugar with the vanilla. Spread the meringue on top of the lemon mixture and bake the pie in heated oven for 15 minutes or until the topping is lightly browned. Chill before serving.

Note: all quantities given here are for 2 servings only.

Eggs Florentine

4 eggs
$\frac{3}{4}$–1 lb fresh spinach or
   1 package frozen spinach
2 tablespoons butter
pinch of ground nutmeg
salt and pepper
1 tablespoon vinegar
   (for poaching)
2 tablespoons heavy cream
2–3 slices of bread, crusts
   removed, cut in triangles and
   fried in 3–4 tablespoons
   oil and butter, mixed (for
   croûtes)

Method
Wash fresh spinach thoroughly, discard the stems and cook it in boiling salted water for 5 minutes or until tender; cook frozen spinach according to package directions. Drain the spinach, press it between 2 plates to remove all water, then chop it.

In a saucepan melt the butter, add the spinach and heat, stirring, until all moisture has evaporated. Add the nutmeg and seasoning, cover and keep warm.

To poach the eggs: fill a shallow saucepan or deep skillet two-thirds full with boiling water and add the vinegar. Bring the water to a rolling boil and break an egg into a briskly bubbling patch — the bubbles will spin the egg so the white sets around the yolk. Repeat with the remaining eggs, then turn down the heat and simmer the eggs very gently for 3–4 minutes or until the whites are firm and the yolks are still soft. Lift out the eggs with a slotted spoon and drain thoroughly.

Meanwhile, stir the cream into the spinach and spread it on a platter. Set the eggs on top, arrange the croûtes around the edge and serve at once.

Mexican Chicken

4 chicken pieces
1–2 teaspoons chili powder
1 tablespoon flour
3 tablespoons olive oil
2 onions, finely sliced
2 cups (1 lb) canned Italian-
   type plum tomatoes
2 cloves of garlic, crushed
bouquet garni
salt and pepper
hot tortillas (to serve) –
   optional

Method
Roll the chicken pieces in a mixture of the chili powder and flour.

In a flameproof casserole heat the oil and fry the chicken pieces over moderate heat until golden brown on all sides. Take them out, add the onions and cook until golden.

Add the tomatoes, garlic, bouquet garni and salt and pepper and put back the chicken, pushing the pieces well into the tomato mixture. Bring to a boil and simmer very gently, stirring occasionally, for 30–40 minutes or until the chicken is tender.

Remove the bouquet garni and serve the chicken with hot tortillas (fresh, canned or frozen).

Melon Compote

2–3 cups melon balls, cut from
   cantaloupe, honeydew or
   Persian melon
grated rind and juice of $\frac{1}{2}$ lemon
$\frac{1}{4}$ cup orange juice
$\frac{1}{4}$ cup light corn syrup
2 tablespoons Curaçao or
   Grand Marnier

Method
In a pan simmer the lemon rind and juice, orange juice and corn syrup for 2 minutes. Pour the hot mixture over the melon balls and let stand 1 hour. Drain and boil the syrup until thick. Cool, pour it over the melon balls, add the liqueur and chill.

Storing Melon
When storing melon in the refrigerator be sure to keep it cut side down and in an airtight wrap as it quickly transfers its flavor to other foods, especially milk.

Grapefruit Mousse

1 can (6 oz) frozen concentrated
   grapefruit juice
1 egg white
3 tablespoons sugar

2 sherbet glasses

Method
Take the can of grapefruit juice from the freezer about 1 hour before needed — it should be slushy when opened.

Beat the egg white until it holds a stiff peak, add the sugar and continue to beat until the mixture is firm. Gradually add the grapefruit juice, beating constantly — if possible, do this with an electric mixer.

Spoon the mousse into the sherbet glasses and chill well before serving.

Note: all quantities given here are for 2 servings only.

Eggs Florentine — poached eggs are served on a bed of spinach purée and garnished with croûtes

Avocado salad is a simple and refreshing appetizer

Menu 6

Avocado Salad

Chicken Breasts
with Mushrooms
Risi-Bisi

Fresh Pineapple
macerated with
Rum and Sugar

Avocado Salad

1 avocado ($\frac{1}{2}$ per person)
1 tablespoon chopped green
    pepper
1 tablespoon chopped green
    onion
3 ripe olives, pitted and
    chopped
watercress (for garnish)

For vinaigrette dressing
salt
black pepper, freshly ground
$\frac{3}{4}$ tablespoon white wine
    vinegar
2$\frac{1}{2}$ tablespoons oil
lemon juice (to taste)
sugar (to taste)
1 teaspoon chopped parsley

This recipe was first given in
Volume 2.

Method
Blanch chopped green pep-
per by boiling in water for 1
minute, draining, and rinsing
in cold water.

To make dressing, mix a
generous pinch of salt and
black pepper with vinegar;
beat in oil. Add enough lemon
juice to sharpen dressing,
sugar to taste, and parsley;
stir in green pepper, onions
and olives.

Cut avocado in half lengthwise, remove seed and brush
the exposed flesh with lemon
juice to prevent it from browning. Fill each cavity with
dressing and chill avocado
slightly before serving on
individual salad plates. Garnish with watercress. Alternatively, peel avocado and
serve, rounded side up, with
dressing spooned over.

Chicken Breasts
with Mushrooms

2–4 chicken breasts
1 carrot, sliced
1 onion, sliced
1 cup chicken stock or water
1$\frac{1}{2}$ tablespoons butter
1$\frac{1}{2}$ tablespoons flour
$\frac{1}{2}$ cup (2 oz) mushrooms, sliced
    and sautéed in 1 tablespoon
    butter
2 egg yolks
$\frac{1}{2}$ cup heavy cream

Method
Put the chicken breasts in a
small pan with the carrot,
onion and stock or water.
Cover and simmer very gently
for 30–35 minutes or until
the chicken is tender. Drain
and cut the meat in one piece
from the bone; discard the
bone. Lay the meat on a platter and keep warm. Strain the
stock.

In a saucepan melt the
butter, stir in the flour and
cook until straw-colored. Pour
on the stock and bring the
sauce to a boil, stirring. Simmer 2 minutes and add the
mushrooms.

In a bowl mix the egg yolks
with the cream and stir in a
little of the hot sauce. Stir
this liaison back into the
remaining sauce, off the heat,
and heat gently until it thickens slightly. Do not boil. Taste
for seasoning, spoon over the
chicken and serve.

Risi-Bisi

$\frac{1}{2}$ cup rice
salt and pepper
2 tablespoons butter
small package of frozen peas,
    cooked

Method
Cook the rice in plenty of boiling salted water for 12 minutes or until tender. Drain and
wash it with hot water to
remove the starch.

Melt the butter in a skillet,
add the rice and toss with a
fork until very hot and season
to taste. Add the peas and stir
1 minute until hot.

Fresh Pineapple
macerated with
Rum and Sugar

1 small pineapple, peeled and
    cut (see below)
2 tablespoons rum (or to taste)
3–4 tablespoons sugar (or to
    taste)

Method
Put the pineapple slices in
a bowl, pour over the rum and
sprinkle on the sugar. Cover
and leave to macerate in the
refrigerator for at least 1 hour
before serving.

To Peel and Cut
Fresh Pineapple
Slice off bottom of pineapple
with serrated-edge knife. Hold
pineapple firmly and with a
sharp stainless steel knife cut
down between 'eyes' at a 45°
angle. The pineapple eyes
should come out easily in
strips. Remove the plume,
slice flesh thinly and cut out
the core with an apple corer.
This method of peeling and
coring disposes of the 'eyes'
but avoids waste.

Note: all quantities given
here are for 2 servings only.

PRESERVES (2)

The later produce of summer — tomatoes, peppers, apples, plums — continues in abundance until fall, unlike the early summer fruits which were discussed in Volume 7. You can preserve your choice at leisure of jams and butters, sweet or sour pickles, chutneys and sauces ready for the table. Line your shelves with the perfect accompaniment or garnish for almost every dish — from bread to curries, cold meats or game.

If you have not made jam or jelly before, refer to the general rules for preserving that were given in Volume 7.

To Test Jams or Jellies for Jell Point

Draw the preserving kettle aside, quickly cool a little jam or jelly on a cold plate (or drop a little on the bottom of an ice cube tray taken straight from the freezer).

Run your index finger through the center — if ready, it will crinkle slightly and remain in 2 separate portions. It will also form a firm drop on the finger.

JAMS

Plum Jam

8 lb plums
1 cup sugar, for each cup prepared fruit

This jam is especially rich and full of flavor if it is made with prune or Italian plums. As with all fruits for jam, plums are best when barely ripe — if pits are difficult to remove, wait until the jam is boiling when the pits can easily be skimmed from the surface.

Method
With a stainless steel knife, cut around the plums, twist to halve them and remove the pits. Crack a few of these, take out the kernels and reserve. Tie the remaining pits in a piece of cheesecloth. Measure the fruit and a proportionate amount of sugar needed. Layer the fruit with half the sugar in a glass or enamel bowl and let stand overnight.

Put the fruit and sugar into a preserving kettle, set on a gentle heat and bring slowly to a boil, skimming occasionally. Add the bag of pits and simmer until the plums are just tender.

Warm the remaining sugar in a low oven (250°F). Sprinkle over the warmed sugar, bring to a boil and boil rapidly for 15—20 minutes or until the jam gives a jell test and add the reserved kernels. Cool jam, remove bag of pits and pour into hot, dry jars. Seal when cool.

Watchpoint: because this jam is particularly juicy, it should be cooled until fruit is more or less suspended in syrup before being put in jars, so that fruit does not rise to the top.

Damson Plum Jam

Follow the recipe for plum jam, cutting the fruit in half and layering with sugar as before. Do not attempt to remove the pits but skim off as many as possible when the jam boils.

Pear and Lime Jam

3 lb pears
3 limes
½ cup water
3 cups sugar
2 tablespoons lemon juice

Method
Pare, core and coarsely chop the pears. Halve the limes and slice very thinly, skin and all.

Combine the pears and limes with the water in a preserving kettle, bring to a boil and cook gently for 10—12 minutes.

Warm the sugar in a low oven (250°F). Stir often, add the sugar and lemon juice and boil hard until the jam gives a jell test. Pour the jam into hot, dry jars and seal at once.

Apple Ginger Jam

8 lb tart apples
4 walnut-sized pieces of fresh, or dry ginger root
thinly peeled rind and juice of 2 lemons
12 cups light brown sugar

This jam is excellent in a sandwich with a slice of mild Cheddar cheese.

Method
Finely chop the fresh ginger or bruise dry ginger by pounding in a mortar with a pestle or beating with a rolling pin. Tie the lemon rind and dry ginger in cheesecloth. Add the fresh ginger to the sugar.

Pare, quarter and core the apples and layer them in a bowl with the sugar. Bury the lemon rind and dry ginger (if used) in center. Pour over lemon juice and stand 24 hours.

Put the fruit into a preserving kettle and stir well while bringing to a boil. Boil rapidly for 15—20 minutes, stirring fairly frequently, until the jam gives a jell test. Take out the lemon rind and dry ginger before pouring the jam into hot, dry jars. Seal at once.

JELLIES

Jellies are made with the strained juice of fresh fruit and sugar. Hard fruits or fruits with pits need a small quantity of water when being softened to a pulp to make jelly, although soft fruits like blackberries and red currants produce enough juice during cooking without added water.

It is important to add only a small quantity of water — otherwise the jelly takes too long to reach jell point and, once the sugar is added, long boiling may spoil the color and flavor.

The best jelly is made by cooking small quantities of fruit juice — no more than 4—6 cups at a time.

Damson Plum Jelly

5 lb damson plums
3 cups water
¾—1 cup sugar, for every cup juice

Method
Wash the plums and simmer them in the water until pulpy. Ladle the fruit and liquid into a jelly bag or a clean cloth and leave to drip overnight.

Measure the juice and warm the proportionate amount of sugar in a low oven (250°F). (1 cup per cup of juice if fruit is very tart).

Put the juice and warmed sugar in a preserving kettle, dissolve the sugar over low heat, stirring occasionally, then boil rapidly until it gives a jell test. Pour the jelly into hot, dry jars. Seal and cover when cool.

Cranberry and Apple Jelly

3 quarts cranberries
5 lb tart apples or crab apples
rind of 2 oranges
1 stick of cinnamon
7–8 cups water
1 cup sugar, for every cup
   juice

Method
Wipe the apples or crab apples, cut them in pieces without removing the cores and combine in a preserving kettle with the washed cranberries. Add the orange rind and cinnamon, tied together with string.

Pour in the water, bring the mixture to a boil and cook to a pulp, stirring occasionally. Ladle into a jelly bag or clean cloth suspended on a stand or upturned chair and leave to drip overnight.

Measure the juice and warm the proportionate amount of sugar in a low oven (250°F). Return the warmed sugar and juice to the kettle and cook over low heat until the sugar is dissolved, stirring occasionally. Boil rapidly until the mixture gives a jell test. Pour the jelly into hot, dry jars and seal when cool.

Blackberry and Apple Jelly

Follow recipe for cranberry and apple jelly but use 2 quarts blackberries and 2 lb tart apples. Allow ¾–1 cup warmed sugar for every cup of juice. The apples contain enough pectin to set the jelly well.

Grape Jelly

2 lb Concord grapes
1 tart apple
½ cup water
¾–1 cup sugar, for every cup
   juice

Method
Wash the grapes and pull them from the stems. Quarter the apple and combine it with the grapes and water in a preserving kettle.

Bring the mixture to a boil and simmer until very soft, stirring occasionally. Ladle this mixture into a jelly bag or a clean dry cloth and leave to drip overnight.

Measure the juice, warm the proportionate amount of sugar in a low oven (250°F). The amount of sugar depends on the acidity of the grapes. Boil the juice rapidly for 5 minutes, skim all foam from the top and add the sugar. Stir until it is dissolved, then boil rapidly until the mixture gives a jell test. Pour the jelly into hot, dry jars; seal and cover when cold.

FRUIT BUTTERS

Butters are fruit purées which are boiled with sugar until very thick, as in making jam. When cooled they set to a thick but spreadable consistency or, if you like, they can be cooked further so that they set to a firm, close mixture which can be cut in slices with a knife.

Either way, fruit butters are delicious with crackers, cottage cheese or as an accompaniment to cold meats. They should be made with strongly flavored fruits because the long cooking necessary to thicken the butter destroys delicate flavors.

If cooking over direct heat, butters must be stirred often to prevent sticking; they also tend to sputter. To avoid both these hazards, you can cook them in a low oven (300°F) where they will need little attention until the end of cooking time when you must keep an eye on them. Store butters in small jars so they are used quickly as they tend to dry out once opened.
Note: after cooking, pour fruit butters into hot, dry jars and seal at once.

Apple Butter

5 lb tart apples
7 cups water
2 cups cider
4 cups sugar
1 tablespoon cinnamon
1 teaspoon ground cloves
1 teaspoon allspice
½ teaspoon nutmeg

Method
Wash and cut the apples in quarters. Cook them in the water in a preserving kettle for about 15 minutes or until the apples are soft. Work them through a fine sieve or a food mill; they should make about 2 quarts purée.

Boil the cider until it is reduced by half and add it to the apple purée with the sugar and all the spices. Return the mixture to the kettle and bring to a boil. Reduce the heat and simmer the mixture over low heat, stirring frequently, or bake in a low oven (300°F) until it is thick and dark.

Peach or Nectarine Butter

Pour boiling water over peaches or nectarines, leave 15 seconds and drain off the water. Peel and pit the fruit.

Put the fruit in a preserving kettle with just enough water to prevent it from sticking and cook until soft, stirring occasionally.

Press the fruit through a fine sieve or purée in a blender and measure.

To each cup of purée add ½ cup sugar. Return the mixture to the kettle and cook over low heat, stirring frequently, or bake in a low oven (300°F) until it is thick and clear. If you like, add ground cinnamon or cloves to taste.

Pear Butter

Wash and slice ripe pears and cook them in a preserving kettle with just enough water to keep them from sticking, stirring occasionally until soft.

Press the pears through a fine sieve and measure the purée.

To 6 cups pear purée add 3 cups sugar, ¼ cup orange juice, 1 teaspoon grated orange rind and ¼ teaspoon ground cloves. Return the mixture to the kettle, bring to a boil and continue cooking over low heat, stirring frequently, or bake in a low oven (300°F) until the mixture is thick.

Plum Butter

Wash Italian or prune plums, cut them in quarters and discard the pits. Cook the plums in a preserving kettle with $\frac{1}{4}$ inch water until they are very tender. Work them through a fine sieve or purée in a blender.

For every 2 cups purée, add 1 cup brown sugar, 1 teaspoon ground cloves, 1 teaspoon allspice and 1 teaspoon cinnamon. Return the mixture to the kettle, bring to a boil, lower the heat and simmer over low heat, stirring frequently, or bake in a low oven (300°F) until it thickens.

Grape Butter

Wash Concord grapes and remove the stems. Put the grapes in a preserving kettle with $\frac{1}{4}$ inch water and simmer until tender. Work the mixture through a sieve to remove the seeds and skins.

Measure the purée and for every cup add $\frac{1}{2}$ cup sugar. Return to the kettle, bring to a boil, lower the heat and simmer the purée over a moderate heat, stirring frequently, or bake in a low oven (300°F) until it thickens.

The ingredients for chutneys are cooked together gently with vinegar, spices and sugar until very thick when the mixture should just drop easily from a spoon. Consistency is important as a chutney that is slightly undercooked will not keep well. Often the main ingredients for a chutney are lightly salted and left overnight as for pickles. However, for some chutneys like pear and tomato this is not necessary.

Seal the chutney carefully to prevent evaporation and store in a cool place. The flavor of chutneys improves enormously with keeping.

Ripe Tomato Chutney

6 lb ripe tomatoes
6 onions, thinly sliced or chopped
6 green peppers, cored, seeded and sliced
2 cups white vinegar
1 cup dark brown sugar
2 tablespoons salt (or to taste)
grated rind and juice of 2 lemons
grated rind and juice of 1 orange
1 teaspoon ground mace
1 teaspoon ground black pepper
1 teaspoon ground ginger

Method
Scald and peel the tomatoes, core them, cut in half and squeeze to remove most of the seeds. Strain these and put the liquid from them into an enamel or stainless steel pan with the tomatoes.

Add the remaining ingredients, stir well, bring to a boil and simmer $1-1\frac{1}{2}$ hours or until thick, stirring occasion-

ally. When really thick and rich, spoon the chutney into small hot, dry jars. Cool and seal when cold.

Apple and Tomato Chutney

4 lb tart apples
4 lb ripe tomatoes, peeled and sliced
4 onions, sliced
5 cups white wine or cider vinegar
2 teaspoons peppercorns
1 tablespoon ground ginger
2 tablespoons salt
2 cups dark brown sugar

Method
Put the tomatoes into a large bowl with the onions, pour over the vinegar and add the peppercorns tied in a cheesecloth bag, ginger, salt and sugar. Cover and leave overnight in a cool place.

Pare, core and slice the apples and combine them with the tomato mixture in an enamel or stainless steel pan. Heat until the sugar is dissolved, bring to a boil, stirring frequently, and simmer about $1\frac{1}{2}$ hours or until the mixture is thick and pulpy. Remove the peppercorns and spoon the chutney into small hot, dry jars. Cool, and seal when cold.

Green peppers are thinly sliced for ripe tomato chutney

After long simmering, tomato chutney should be dark and quite thick

PICKLES

Fruits and vegetables for pickling must be of top quality. Most vegetables are washed, then salted or soaked in brine. Pickling salt or Kosher salt rather than iodized table salt is best for this purpose.

After salting, vegetables are rinsed, then packed into glass jars or crocks, preferably with glass tops to avoid corrosion, and covered with spiced vinegar.

The type of vinegar – cider, wine, white or tarragon – depends on the pickle; it must be top quality to be certain it contains the amount of acetic acid needed to preserve the vegetables.

Because of the vinegar content, pickles should be cooked in an enamel or stainless steel pan or preserving kettle; aluminum discolors the pickles.

Pickles should be stored in a cool, dark, dry place – 50°F–55°F is ideal. If the temperature is too high they will deteriorate rapidly. Pickles improve and mellow with keeping – mild pickles should be used within 2–3 months, but spicy mixtures can be kept 6 months or more.

Piccalilli

2 quarts green tomatoes
$\frac{3}{8}$ cup salt
$\frac{1}{2}$ teaspoon pepper
1 teaspoon dry mustard
1 teaspoon ground cinnamon
1 teaspoon ground allspice
1 teaspoon ground cloves
$\frac{1}{4}$ cup white mustard seed
1 teaspoon celery seed
2 cups white vinegar
2 green peppers, cored, seeded and chopped
3 large onions, chopped
3 cups sugar

Method

Coarsely chop the tomatoes, sprinkle them with salt and leave overnight. Drain well.

Combine the spices and vinegar in an enamel or stainless steel pan and bring to a boil. Add the tomatoes, peppers, onions and sugar to the pan, stir until the sugar is dissolved and bring to a boil. Simmer 30 minutes or until thick, stirring occasionally. Pack the pickle into hot, dry jars and seal at once.

Spiced Vinegar

1 quart white vinegar
2 teaspoons peppercorns
1 teaspoon whole allspice
1 teaspoon mustard seed
2 blades of mace
1 stick of cinnamon

Method

Tie the spices in cheesecloth and combine with the vinegar in an enamel or stainless steel pan. Cover and bring slowly to a boil. When just at boiling point, take from the heat and leave for about 2 hours so the vinegar is thoroughly flavored with spices.

Remove the bag of spices and, if not using the vinegar immediately, store in bottles.

Pickled Mushrooms

12 cups (3 lb) mushrooms
$1\frac{1}{2}$ tablespoons salt
1 teaspoon cayenne
1 quart spiced vinegar (see left)

Method

Trim the stems of the mushrooms level with the caps so they keep a good shape. Wipe them with a damp cloth, if necessary, but do not wash them. Spread them on a tray, sprinkle with the salt and leave 30 minutes.

Put the mushrooms in a pan, add the cayenne and cook over very low heat until the juice begins to run; increase the heat and cook 4–5 minutes. Pour on enough spiced vinegar barely to cover, simmer 10–12 minutes, then cool in this liquid.

Lift the mushrooms out with a slotted spoon and put them in small, hot and dry jars. Bring the liquid to a boil and pour over the mushrooms to cover. Seal at once and keep 1–2 weeks before using.

Pickling salt, fine-grained and pure with no additives, is particularly good for pickles because it leaves no cloudy residue when dissolved.

Pickled Red Cabbage

1 medium head of red cabbage
about 3 tablespoons salt
1 quart spiced vinegar (see left)

Method

Quarter the cabbage and shred it finely, discarding the hard stalk. Spread it on a tray, sprinkle with salt, cover and leave 24 hours in a cool place.

Watchpoint: do not worry if the cabbage turns blue; it will return to its normal red color after being covered with the spiced vinegar.

Rinse the cabbage quickly with cold water. Pack it into hot and dry screwtop jars, cover with spiced vinegar and seal at once. Leave for a week before eating. If kept for longer than 2–3 months, the cabbage will lose its crispness.

Pickling spice is a mixture of whole spices (peppercorns, allspice, mace, etc.) and is a convenient way of buying spices if you do not often use them.

Mustard Pickle

4 cucumbers, peeled and cut in
    chunks
1 lb small onions, peeled
4 medium zucchini, trimmed
    and thickly sliced
1 large cauliflower, divided
    into flowerets
$\frac{1}{2}$ lb green beans, trimmed and
    halved
about 3 tablespoons salt

For pickle
5 cups white vinegar
2 tablespoons pickling spice
    (see box)
1 cup dark brown sugar
1 tablespoon turmeric
1 tablespoon dry mustard
1 tablespoon flour

Method

Combine the vegetables in a
bowl (they should be in even
pieces), sprinkle with the salt,
cover and stand in a cool place
for 12 hours. Drain.

In a pan boil 3 cups vinegar
with the pickling spice for 5
minutes and strain. Stir
remaining vinegar into the
sugar, turmeric, mustard and
flour and combine this mixture in the pan with the strained vinegar. Heat until the
sugar is dissolved, bring to a
boil, stirring, and add the
vegetables. Simmer 10 minutes, take from the heat and
cool. Pack into dry jars, seal
at once and leave 1 month
before using.

Sweet Pickled Onions

3 lb baby onions
3–4 tablespoons salt
few sprigs of fresh tarragon or
    1 teaspoon dried tarragon
2–3 red or green chili peppers
$1\frac{1}{4}$–$1\frac{1}{2}$ cups sugar
5–6 cups white wine or white
    vinegar

Method

Trim the tops and roots from
the onions, taking care not to
cut too much root away or the
onions will fall apart. Put
them in a bowl, cover with
boiling water, count to 20,
drain and cover with cold
water; the skin will peel away
easily. Be sure to keep the
onions under water while
peeling them. Layer them in
a bowl with the salt, cover and
leave in a cool place overnight.

Put the onions in a colander
and rinse well. Shake off as
much liquid as possible and
pack them into dry jars, adding a sprig of fresh tarragon or a
pinch of dried tarragon and
half a chili pepper to each jar.

In a pan, dissolve the sugar
in the vinegar and boil 1 minute. Pour the hot syrup over
the onions to cover them
completely and seal at once.
Leave 2–3 weeks before
using.

Watermelon Rind Pickles

1 large watermelon
4 tablespoons slaked lime
    (available at most
    pharmacies)
4 quarts water
8–10 cups sugar
8 cups white vinegar
2 tablespoons whole allspice
2 tablespoons whole cloves
4 sticks of cinnamon
2 pieces of ginger root

Method

Peel and discard all dark green
skin and pink flesh from the
watermelon. Cut the rind into
cubes or slices and measure
enough to make 4 quarts.
Cook the rind in boiling water
to cover for 5 minutes, drain,
and cool.

Dissolve the slaked lime in
2 quarts of the cold water,
pour it over the rind and let
stand for 3 hours. Drain and
rinse well. Add enough fresh
water to the rind to cover,
bring to a boil and boil 5–6
minutes or until the rind is
tender – a thin skewer should
pierce it easily. Drain well.

In a pan, combine 4 cups of
the sugar, 2 cups vinegar,
remaining 2 quarts water, and
all the spices tied in a cheesecloth bag. Heat until the
sugar is dissolved, bring to a
boil and boil 5 minutes.

Add the rind, bring to a
boil again and simmer 30
minutes. Let the rind stand
in the syrup for 12–24 hours
in a cool place.

Add remaining 6 cups
vinegar, and 4–8 cups sugar
(according to taste) and bring
to a boil. Simmer the rind until
it is transparent. If the syrup
becomes too thick before the
rind is clear, add $\frac{1}{2}$ cup hot
water as needed. Remove the
spice bag and pack the hot
rind and syrup into hot, dry
jars. Seal at once.

Spiced Plums

3 lb prune or Italian plums
1 stick of cinnamon
whole cloves

For syrup
3 cups white or cider vinegar
2 cups sugar

This pickle is especially good
with cold lamb or veal.

Method

Wash the plums and prick
them all over with a skewer
or toothpick. Pack them into
screwtop jars and add a small
piece of cinnamon and 2 cloves
to each jar.

In a pan combine the vinegar and sugar and heat until
the sugar is dissolved. Bring
to a boil and boil 6–7 minutes.
Pour the hot syrup over the
plums. Cool, then seal the
lids and store for about 1
month before using.

Pickled Peppers

12 green or red peppers
1 quart white vinegar
1 cup water
1 tablespoon salt
3 cloves of garlic
$\frac{1}{2}$ cup brown sugar

Method

Quarter the peppers, removing
the core and all the seeds.
Blanch them in boiling water
for 2 minutes and drain thoroughly. Pack them into hot,
dry jars.

In a pan combine the vinegar, water, salt, garlic and
sugar; heat until sugar is
dissolved. Bring to a boil and
simmer 5 minutes. Pour over
the peppers and seal at once.
This pickle will keep for 6
months.

For pickled pears, the pears are poached, then simmered in spiced vinegar syrup until tender

Pickled Pears

8 lb unripe pears
1 stick of cinnamon
3–4 whole cloves
7 cups sugar
5 cups white wine or white
   vinegar

Method

Tie the spices in a piece of cheesecloth and combine in a pan with the sugar and vinegar. Heat until the sugar is dissolved, bring to a boil and set aside.

Pare the pears, quarter and core them, or leave them whole if very small. Put them in a pan, barely cover with cold water, bring to a boil and simmer, covered, for 15–30 minutes or until almost tender; the cooking time depends very much on the type and ripeness of the pears.

Drain and put the pears into the spiced syrup. Bring to a boil and simmer very gently until the pears look transparent and are very tender – this may take up to 1 hour, depending on the pears. Lift them out with a slotted spoon, and pack into jars.

Boil the syrup until it thickens slightly and pour it over the pears to cover them completely. Seal at once and leave 1 month before using.

Pickled Walnuts

green walnuts
½ cup salt for every 5 cups
   water (for brine)

For spiced vinegar
for every 5 cups white vinegar,
   add 2 tablespoons
   peppercorns, 2 walnut-sized
   pieces of dried ginger root
   and 2 tablespoons whole
   allspice

If you have a walnut tree, try this unusual English recipe that uses green walnuts. They should be picked in June or July, before the shell has formed and can harden in the pickle. If you push a thin skewer or knitting needle into the nut, you will be able to feel when the shell is beginning to form. Be sure to wear rubber gloves as walnuts stain badly.

Pickled walnuts are generally served with cold meats and are an excellent alternative to ripe olives for decoration.

Method

For the brine: boil the water and pour in the salt. Stir well to dissolve and cool before using.

Wearing rubber gloves, prick the walnuts all over with a thin skewer or metal knitting needle. Put them into a bowl and cover with brine. Put a plate on top of the walnuts to keep them under the surface and leave 5–6 days in a cool place. Drain them, cover again with fresh brine and leave for another week.

Drain the walnuts well, spread them on a tray and leave in a warm room or, better still, in the sun. Turn them occasionally and leave for 2–3 days or until they turn black.

To make the spiced vinegar: crush the spices lightly to bruise them, tie in a piece of cheesecloth and add to the vinegar. Boil in a covered enamel or stainless steel pan for 10 minutes. Cool and remove the spices.

Pack the walnuts into dry jars, then cover with spiced vinegar. Seal and leave them 7–8 weeks before using.

Sweet Cucumber Pickle

20 cucumbers, peeled and
   sliced
1½ lb small onions, thinly sliced
2 green peppers, cored, seeded
   and cut in strips
¼ cup salt

For pickle
4 cups white wine or white
   vinegar
2 cups granulated or light
   brown sugar
¼ cup mustard seed
2 teaspoons celery seed
2 teaspoons turmeric
1 teaspoon ground mace

Method

Layer the cucumbers, onions and peppers in a bowl and sprinkle with the salt. Cover and leave 2–3 hours in a cool place. Put into a colander, rinse with cold water and drain.

To make the pickle: combine all the ingredients in a shallow enamel or stainless steel pan and stir well. Heat until the sugar is dissolved, bring to a boil, and boil 3 minutes. Take from the heat, add the vegetables and shake the pan well to mix thoroughly.

Bring just back to a boil, stirring from time to time to make sure all the vegetables are covered with the hot liquid. Take from heat, cool, spoon into dry jars and seal.

Sweet Dill Pickles

6 large dill pickles
2 cups sugar
½ cup tarragon vinegar
3 cloves of garlic, cut in half
2 tablespoons pickling spice
   (see page 36)

Method

Cut the dill pickles in ¼-inch slices and pack in dry jars.

In an enamel or stainless steel pan combine the sugar, vinegar, garlic and the pickling spice tied in a cheesecloth bag. Heat until the sugar is dissolved, bring the mixture to a boil and let cool. Discard the spice bag and pour the cool pickling liquid over the pickle slices. Seal and keep in a cool place for at least 1 week to develop the flavor.

Kosher Dill Pickles

4 quarts medium cucumbers
sprigs of fresh dill
cloves of garlic
small fresh red chili peppers
4 cups white vinegar
3 quarts water
1 cup salt

Method

Wash the cucumbers, cover them with cold water and let stand overnight in a cool place.

In the bottom of clean, dry quart jars put a sprig of fresh dill and pack in the cucumbers carefully. To each jar add a garlic clove, a chili pepper and another sprig of dill.

In an enamel or stainless steel pan, heat together the vinegar, water and salt until it comes to a vigorous boil. Fill the jars with the pickling liquid, seal them and store for at least 5 days before eating.

Sweet Green Tomato Pickle

4 lb small, even-sized green
  tomatoes
2 cups white or white wine
  vinegar
1 teaspoon salt
1 quart water

For pickle
4 cups sugar
1½ cups wine vinegar
3 cups water
2 fresh or 3 dried red chili
  peppers
8–10 whole cloves

Method
Remove all stems and wipe the tomatoes. Prick them all over with a fork and put in a heat-proof bowl.

In a pan bring the vinegar, salt and 1 quart water to a boil, pour over the tomatoes and cover them with a plate to keep them submerged.

To make the pickle: in a shallow enamel or stainless steel pan heat the sugar until dissolved in the vinegar and water with the spices (tied in a cheesecloth bag), bring to a boil and boil 7–8 minutes — the liquid should be syrupy.

Lift the tomatoes from the salt and vinegar liquid with a slotted spoon, add them to the pickle syrup and simmer until barely tender, turning them from time to time so they cook evenly.

Lift them out carefully and pack in hot and dry, wide-necked glass jars. Remove the spices in the cheesecloth bag, boil the syrup until quite thick and pour over the tomatoes. Seal at once.
Watchpoint: when simmering the tomatoes in the pickle, use a shallow pan so the tomatoes can spread out.

Ripe Tomato Pickle

7 lb ripe tomatoes
⅓ cup salt or brine (to cover)

For brine (optional)
2½ quarts boiling water
⅔ cup salt

For pickle
3 cloves of garlic, chopped
4½ cups dark brown sugar
6 cups white vinegar
3 blades of mace
2 tablespoons whole allspice
2 sticks of cinnamon

Method
First make the brine (if using): add salt to boiling water, stir to dissolve, and cool.

Wipe the tomatoes and cut them in thick slices, removing any blemishes. Layer them in a large bowl with the salt or, if you prefer, barely cover them with brine. Leave for 24 hours, then drain thoroughly.

To make the pickle: in an enamel or stainless steel pan combine garlic, sugar and vinegar. Heat until the sugar is dissolved, bring to a boil and add the spices, tied in a piece of cheesecloth.

Add the tomatoes, shake the pan and bring back to the boil slowly. Simmer for 3 minutes, turning the tomatoes with a slotted spatula to prevent them from breaking too much.

Lift out the tomatoes carefully and pack them into hot, dry jars. Boil the remaining pickle syrup rapidly for about 15 minutes or until thick, remove the cheesecloth bag, and pour the syrup over the tomatoes while still hot. Cool and seal.

SPICED FRUIT SAUCES

Fruit sauces and ketchups are thinner than chutneys and are smoother in consistency. Like chutneys, they improve on keeping.

Cranberry Ketchup

2½ lb cranberries
cider vinegar
2½ cups sugar
1 tablespoon cinnamon
1 teaspoon ground cloves

Method
Wash the cranberries, put them in a kettle and add enough vinegar just to cover. Bring to a boil and cook 8–10 minutes or until the cranberries are tender.

Work the mixture through a fine sieve or purée in a blender and mix the purée with the sugar and the spices.

Heat gently until the sugar is dissolved, then simmer this ketchup, stirring frequently, until it is thick. Pour into hot, dry bottles and seal.

Plum Sauce

2 lb prune or Italian plums,
  pitted
6 large onions, thinly sliced
¾ cup golden raisins
½ tablespoon crushed dried
  chili peppers
1 walnut-sized piece of dry
  ginger root, crushed
5 cups white wine or white
  vinegar
1 cup granulated or light
  brown sugar
3 tablespoons salt
½ tablespoon turmeric
½ tablespoon ground nutmeg
2 tablespoons dry mustard
1 tablespoon ground allspice

Method
Put the plums, onions, golden raisins, chili peppers and ginger into an enamel or stainless steel pan with half the vinegar. Bring to a boil and simmer about 30 minutes.

Work the mixture through a sieve or food mill and return to the pan with the sugar, salt, turmeric, nutmeg, mustard and allspice. Add the remaining vinegar and simmer 30 minutes longer, stirring frequently or until the mixture is the consistency of thick cream. Leave until cold, pour into dry jars or bottles and seal.

Spiced Chili Sauce

4 quarts ripe tomatoes
1 cup chopped onions
1½ cups chopped sweet red
   peppers
1½ cups chopped green peppers
1½ teaspoons whole allspice
1½ teaspoons whole cloves
2 sticks of cinnamon
2 cups vinegar
1 cup sugar
3 tablespoons salt

Method
Peel and chop tomatoes and put them in an enamel or stainless steel pan with the onions and both red and green peppers. Tie the spices in a cheesecloth bag, add to the vegetables and bring the mixture to a boil. Cook over moderate heat until the mixture is reduced by half, stirring frequently.

Add the vinegar, sugar and salt. When the sugar has dissolved, boil vigorously for 5 minutes, stirring constantly. Discard the spice bag and pour the chili sauce into hot, dry jars and seal.

RELISHES

Relishes are cooked for a shorter time than chutneys; to be at their best they should be eaten within 1–2 weeks.

Pear Relish

3 lb pears
1½ lb small white onions
7 green peppers
1 sweet red pepper
¼ cup salt
2 cups sugar
2 cups white vinegar
1 tablespoon mustard seed
1 teaspoon turmeric
¼ teaspoon cayenne pepper

Method
Pare and core the pears and work them through the medium blade of a grinder. Measure 5 cups of pear purée into a large bowl.

Peel the onions; remove the seeds and core from the peppers and work the vegetables through the medium blade of a grinder. Measure 6½ cups of the mixture and combine it with the pears and the salt. Let stand for about 4 hours, then drain well.

In a large enamel or stainless steel pan combine the remaining ingredients, heat until the sugar is dissolved, then bring to a boil. Boil for 5 minutes and add the pear mixture. Simmer for 5 minutes, spoon into hot, dry jars and seal.

Sweet Pepper Relish

6 large green peppers
6 large red peppers
6 medium onions, chopped
3 cups white wine or white
   vinegar
1½ tablespoons salt
1¼ cups sugar
1½ teaspoons mustard seed

Method
Halve the peppers, removing the core and seeds. Finely chop the flesh or put it through a grinder. Combine it with the onions in a bowl, pour on enough boiling water to cover and drain at once.

Put the onion and pepper mixture in an enamel or stainless steel pan, cover with cold water, bring to a boil and drain again.

Put the vinegar, salt, sugar and mustard seed into the pan, heat until the sugar is dissolved and bring to a boil. Stir the drained pepper mixture into the hot vinegar. Simmer 20–25 minutes until it is fairly thick, but not as thick as chutney. Spoon the relish into hot, dry jars and seal.

Mustard Relish

2 quarts green tomatoes
7 large onions
6 yellow or green peppers
6 sweet red peppers
¼ cup salt
2 small bunches of celery,
   finely chopped
2 cups cider vinegar
2 cups sugar
2 tablespoons prepared
   mustard
1 teaspoon turmeric
¼ cup flour
½ cup water

Method
Wash the tomatoes, peel the onions and remove the seeds and core from the peppers. Work the tomatoes and onions through the medium blade of a grinder and mix in 2 tablespoons salt. Grind the peppers into a separate bowl and stir in the remaining 2 tablespoons salt. Let the vegetables stand in a cool place overnight.

Next day drain the vegetables well and put them in an enamel or stainless steel pan with celery, vinegar, sugar, mustard and turmeric. Heat until the sugar is dissolved, bring the relish to a boil and simmer for 15 minutes.

Make a smooth paste of the flour and water and gradually stir it into the hot relish. Simmer 10 minutes longer, stirring frequently, pour into hot, dry jars and seal.

Braised tongues Florentine are garnished with spinach molds and served with a rich brown sauce

SIMPLE INGREDIENTS MAKE A SPECIAL DINNER

Eggs Dijonnaise

Braised Tongues Florentine
Spinach Molds

Apple Chartreuse
with Rum & Apricot Sauce
or Dessert Sour Cream Sauce
or
Cumberland Pudding
with Pineapple Sauce

Red wine – Chianti Classico (Italy)
or Pinot St. George (California)

The town of Florence, Italy, has provided the world with many wonders, including wines. Chianti, the principal wine, has become so famous that many people regard it as the generic appellation for all Italian reds.

Unfortunately, most wine sold as Chianti has little in common with the admirable vintages from the classic Chianti vineyards south of Florence. These can be recognized by their Bordeaux-type bottles (no straw wrapping) and the figure of a black rooster in a small circle on the neck band. Chianti Classicos are widely distributed here, but if you want an American counterpart, try a Pinot St. George from Northern California. Both wines go well with this week's entrée of tongue and its popular partner — spinach.

TIMETABLE

Day before
Make the apple chartreuse, cover and store in mold in refrigerator.

Make mayonnaise and store in airtight container in refrigerator.

Cook tongues, skin, cover and refrigerate.

Morning
Hard cook the eggs and prepare filling.

Prepare mushroom salad.

Prepare all vegetables.

Cook and purée the spinach, prepare béchamel mixture for filling and put into spinach-lined molds or cups ready for baking.

Braise the tongues and make the sauce. Reduce cooking liquid and complete sauce. Put cooked tongues in a clean cold pan and cover with sauce ready to reheat.

Make apricot and rum sauce or dessert sour cream sauce for chartreuse — *or make pineapple sauce for Cumberland pudding;* cover and refrigerate.

Assemble equipment for final cooking from 6.45 p.m. for dinner around 8 p.m.

You will find that **cooking times** given in the individual recipes for these dishes have sometimes been adapted in the timetable to help you when cooking and serving this menu as a party meal.

Order of Work

6.45
Make Cumberland pudding and pour into pan ready for baking.

7:00
Set oven at 350°F. Turn out chartreuse from mold onto a platter.

7:15
Put spinach molds and tongues in oven.

Cook potatoes.

Fill the egg whites, reshape, arrange stuffed eggs on a platter and coat with mayonnaise. Garnish with mushroom salad.

7:40
Turn oven to low and keep spinach molds warm.

Drain potatoes and mash with butter, pour over hot milk to cover; put lid on pan and let stand at back of stove to keep warm.

7:50
Set oven at 375°F and bake Cumberland pudding. Reheat pineapple sauce just before serving.

Slice tongues and keep sauce warm.

Beat potatoes with milk, pile on the platter, arrange slices of tongue on top, cover with foil and return to warm oven.

8:00
Serve appetizer.

After serving the appetizer, turn out the spinach molds and arrange them around the tongues.

Boil the sauce and spoon some over the tongues. Serve the rest separately.

Appetizer

Eggs Dijonnaise

6 hard-cooked eggs
½ cup grated sharp Cheddar cheese
1 cup mayonnaise
salt and pepper
1–2 teaspoons Dijon-style or prepared mustard
1–2 tablespoons light cream or milk

For mushroom salad
2 cups (½ lb) mushrooms, thickly sliced
3 tablespoons olive oil
1 shallot, finely chopped
1 tablespoon chopped parsley
1 tablespoon red wine vinegar

Method
Cut the hard-cooked eggs in half lengthwise, remove the yolks and work them through a sieve into a bowl; keep the whites in a bowl of cold water to prevent them from hardening.

To make the mushroom salad: heat the oil in a skillet, add the mushrooms and shallot and cook briskly for 1 minute only. Transfer the mushroom mixture to a bowl, add the parsley, wine vinegar and seasoning and let stand until cool.

Mix the egg yolks with the grated cheese, add 1–2 tablespoons of mayonnaise to bind the mixture and beat until smooth and creamy. Season to taste.

Dry the egg whites with paper towels and fill them with cheese mixture. Join the halves together and arrange them on a platter.

Add mustard to taste to the remaining mayonnaise and thin it to a thick coating consistency with a little cream or milk — if it is too thin it will slide off the smooth eggs.

Spoon the mustard mayonnaise over eggs and garnish with mushroom salad.

Add the wine vinegar to the mushroom salad; keep the halved egg whites in a bowl of cold water to prevent them from hardening

Beat the oil very slowly into the egg yolk mixture for the mayonnaise. Mix egg yolks with the cheese while mushroom salad is cooling

Eggs Dijonnaise, with mustard-flavored mayonnaise, are garnished with mushroom salad

Mayonnaise

To make 1 cup: in a bowl beat with a small whisk or wooden spoon 2 egg yolks with $\frac{1}{4}$ teaspoon salt, a pinch each of pepper and dry mustard until thick.

Measure $\frac{3}{4}$ cup oil. Add 2 tablespoons oil to the egg yolks drop by drop; the mix-
ture will then be very thick. Stir in 1 teaspoon wine vinegar. The remaining oil can be added more quickly (1 tablespoon at a time, beaten thoroughly between each addition until smooth, or in a thin steady stream if using a blender).

When all the oil has been added, add 1½ tablespoons
more wine vinegar with more seasoning to taste. To thin and lighten mayonnaise, add a little hot water. For a coating consistency, thin with a little cream or milk.

Watchpoint: mayonnaise curdles very easily, so add the oil drop by drop at first until the mixture thickens; then add it in a slow steady stream.
If mayonnaise curdles, start with a fresh yolk in another bowl and work well with seasonings. Then add the curdled mixture drop by drop. Be sure all ingredients are at room temperature before starting.

Entrée

Braised Tongues Florentine

2 calves' tongues or 1 beef
   tongue (1½–2 lb)
3 slices of bacon
2 onions, sliced
2 carrots, sliced
1 stalk of celery, sliced
bouquet garni
6 white peppercorns
1½ cups well-flavored stock

For sauce
2 tablespoons butter
1 shallot or small onion, grated
1½ tablespoons flour
2 cups well-flavored stock
2 teaspoons tomato paste
¼ cup sherry
salt and pepper

For serving
spinach molds
3 medium potatoes, cooked,
   drained and mashed to a
   purée with 1 tablespoon
   butter, ¼ cup hot milk and
   salt and pepper to taste

Method
Blanch, refresh and drain the tongues; put them in a pan with enough cold water to cover and simmer 1½–2 hours for calves' tongues or 2½–3 hours for the beef tongue or until the tongues are very tender. Drain them, plunge in a bowl of cold water and skin them. Trim and cut away the roots and any small bones.

Set oven at moderate (350°F).

Put the bacon slices in the bottom of a flameproof casserole. Add the onions, carrots and celery and cover. Cook mixture over low heat for 10–12 minutes or until the bacon starts to brown.

Put the tongues on top of vegetables and add bouquet garni, peppercorns and 1 cup stock. Cover casserole with foil and the lid and braise in heated oven for 45 minutes.

Watchpoint: braising gives the tongues extra flavor, but they must be quite tender before they are put in the oven.

To prepare the sauce: melt the butter in a saucepan, add shallot or onion and cook slowly for 2 minutes or until soft. Stir in the flour until smooth and continue cooking until the shallot and flour are a deep brown. Take pan from the heat and stir in 1 cup stock with the tomato paste and sherry. Return to the heat and bring to a boil, stirring constantly.

Half cover the pan and simmer 15–20 minutes. Pour in half the remaining stock, skim the sauce and bring to a boil. Reduce heat and simmer 5 minutes. Add remaining stock, skim again, bring to a boil, reduce heat, then simmer 5 minutes longer. Strain and reserve.

Remove the tongues from the casserole and keep warm.

Strain the braising liquid, return it to the pot and boil hard until it is reduced by half. Add the sauce to this liquid, taste for seasoning, bring to a boil and keep warm.

To serve: spoon potato purée down the center of a platter and place the spinach molds around it. Slice the tongues (see box) and arrange them on top of the potatoes. Boil the sauce and spoon just enough over the slices to coat them and the base of the platter. Serve remaining sauce separately.

To Carve a Tongue
Carve in diagonal slices across the tongue, starting at the tip and slanting the knife so the slices are even sized. Small tongues are carved from the tip to the root in 2–4 slices.

Accompaniment to entrée

Spinach Molds

1½ lb fresh leaf spinach,
   thoroughly washed
1 tablespoon butter
béchamel sauce, made with 2
   tablespoons butter,
   2 tablespoons flour and
   1¼ cups milk (infused with
   slice of onion, 6 peppercorns, blade of mace and
   bay leaf)
2 eggs, beaten to mix
salt and pepper
pinch of nutmeg

8 dariole molds or custard cups

Method
Butter the molds or cups. Set the oven at moderate (350°F).

Cook the spinach in boiling salted water for 5 minutes; drain, refresh and press the leaves between 2 plates to remove excess water (the leaves should stay whole and unbroken).

Carefully detach 8 spinach leaves (16 if they are small) and use them to line the buttered molds or cups; work the remaining spinach through a sieve or food mill to make a purée.

Melt the 1 tablespoon butter, cook over low heat until nut-brown, then add spinach purée and cook, stirring, over heat until dry. Stir in the béchamel sauce thoroughly and take from heat.

Alternatively, the spinach can be sautéed in butter, then puréed with the béchamel sauce in a blender.

Beat in the eggs and season well with salt, pepper and a pinch of nutmeg.

Spoon the mixture into the spinach-lined molds or cups, cover with foil and stand them in a water bath. Bake in heated oven for 20–25 minutes or until the molds are firm.

Line the buttered molds with blanched spinach leaves

Beat the eggs into the spinach and béchamel mixture

Dessert

Apple Chartreuse

1 large tart apple such as
   Greening or Granny Smith
5–6 crisp dessert apples such
   as Delicious or McIntosh
1 cup water
1 cup sugar
peeled rind and strained juice
   of 1 lemon
$\frac{3}{4}$ cup chopped mixed candied
   fruit

Soufflé dish (1 quart capacity)

No gelatin is needed because the pectin in the apples is sufficient to set this chartreuse.

Method
Wipe the tart apple with a damp cloth, remove the stem and eye and cut the apple into slices (do not discard the core, peel or seeds).

Put the apple slices into a saucepan with the water, cover and cook gently until the apple is pulpy. Pour the mixture into a strainer over a bowl and let stand, without pressing it, until all the juice has dripped through. Measure 1 cup liquid and put it into a large shallow pan with the sugar, lemon rind and juice.

Cook the mixture over low heat until the sugar has dissolved, boil the juice steadily for 5 minutes, then take the pan from the heat and remove the lemon rind.

Pare and core the dessert apples and cut them immediately into the liquid in even, thin slices about one-eighth inch thick. Cover the pan and cook the apples over low heat for 10–12 minutes or until just tender.

Watchpoint: while cooking, turn the slices once or twice,

taking care not to break them or let the syrup boil — it should simmer very gently.

Then remove the lid and continue cooking until there is just enough syrup left to moisten the apple slices. Remove from the heat and add the candied fruit, cover pan and let the apples stand, off heat, until the slices look clear. Dampen the soufflé dish, carefully pour in the apple mixture and chill 4–6 hours or until set.

To serve: turn the chartreuse out onto a platter and serve with rum and apricot sauce, with dessert sour cream sauce or with heavy cream.

Rum and Apricot Sauce

Combine $\frac{1}{2}$ cup apricot jam, $\frac{1}{4}$ cup water and juice of 1 lemon in a saucepan and heat gently to melt the jam. Bring the sauce to a boil, remove from the heat and stir in 2 tablespoons rum. Work the sauce through a sieve into a bowl and serve cold.

Dessert Sour Cream Sauce

Whip $\frac{1}{2}$ cup heavy cream until it holds a soft shape, then stir in $\frac{1}{2}$ cup sour cream and 1 teaspoon sugar (or to taste).

Thinly slice the pared dessert apples into the pan of syrup, cover and cook until they are tender

Carefully pour the cooled apple slices and candied fruit into the soufflé dish before chilling until set

Apple chartreuse is delicious served with dessert sour cream sauce (recipes are on page 47)

Alternative dessert

Cumberland Pudding

$2\frac{1}{2}$ cups milk
$\frac{1}{4}$ cup butter
$\frac{1}{2}$ cup self-rising flour
pinch of salt
$\frac{1}{4}$ cup sugar
grated rind of 2 lemons
2 eggs, beaten to mix

Quiche pan (1 quart capacity)

Method
Lightly butter the pan; set the oven at moderately hot (375°F).

Cut the butter into the flour in a bowl and rub with the fingertips until the mixture resembles fine crumbs. Stir in the salt, sugar, add the lemon rind and eggs, then stir in the milk.

Pour the mixture into the prepared pan and bake in heated oven for 40–45 minutes or until the mixture is set and lightly browned on top. Serve hot, with pineapple sauce separately.

Pineapple Sauce

Mix 2 tablespoons sugar, 2 teaspoons cornstarch and a pinch of salt together. Stir in $\frac{3}{4}$ cup unsweetened pineapple juice, bring to a boil, stirring, and simmer 2 minutes. Add 1 teaspoon lemon juice and $\frac{3}{4}$ cup fresh or canned crushed pineapple. Serve hot or cold.

Cumberland pudding has a tart pineapple sauce as accompaniment

HOW TO COOK FISH (2)

The fresh fish available in your market depends on where you live but you should be able to find something more interesting than anonymous white fish fillets available almost everywhere. Do not hesitate to take advantage of the fish you find because often recipes can be adapted to suit the different kinds — cod is very much like haddock, for example, and halibut also has a similar texture. Flounder can be used in any recipe calling for sole and small red snapper is a good substitute for mullet.

The most important attribute of any fish is its freshness — look for bright eyes, red gills and shiny skin; fresh fish has little or no odor. Always buy fresh rather than frozen fish whenever possible as freezing is a mixed blessing — it makes fish available in areas where fresh fish is unobtainable but tends to spoil the flavor of delicate kinds like trout.

Fish are versatile — they are good baked, deep or shallow fried, broiled or poached, and go particularly well with sauces — either made from the liquid in which they were cooked or prepared separately with ingredients to contrast with the fish. Fish cooks very quickly and becomes tasteless and dry when overdone. It is done when it flakes easily — when pulled apart gently with a fork, no transparent uncooked flesh can be seen. However, when cooking small fish fillets, a thin transparent line in the center does not matter because the fish will continue cooking for a short time after it is taken from the heat.

Basic methods of cooking fish were given in Volume 2 with recipes for rich fish like mackerel and for white fish, including cod and perch. How to broil fish was described in Volume 3.

FRESH FISH SELECTION

1 Striped Bass (Rock)
2 Halibut
3 Grouper
4 Cod
5 Flounder
6 Black-backed Flounder
7 Norfolk Spot
8 Porgy or Scup
9 Brook Trout

Bass

More than a dozen kinds of bass are found in North American waters. Some are freshwater fish; others, such as striped and sea bass, live in salt water.

Bass are famous game fish and make good eating as they have a rich juicy flesh, though the texture can be rather coarse. Most bass in markets weigh from 2–15 lb; they are sold whole and in fillets.

Small whole bass and fillets can be broiled or fried but larger fish are best baked or poached. A whole striped bass is excellent poached and served hot with hollandaise sauce or cold with green or tomato mayonnaise (as for red snapper recipe on page 60).

Broiled Bass Provençale

1½–2 lb bass fillets
¼ cup olive oil
juice of ½ lemon
salt and pepper

For garnish
2 medium onions, chopped
4 tomatoes, peeled, seeded and chopped
2 cloves of garlic, crushed
3 green peppers, cored, seeded and cut in strips
½ teaspoon oregano
½ teaspoon thyme
1 tablespoon chopped parsley

Method
Mix 2 tablespoons olive oil with lemon juice and seasoning, pour it over the bass, cover and let stand 2–3 hours in refrigerator to marinate. Drain, reserving marinade.

To make the garnish: heat the remaining oil and fry onion until soft. Add tomatoes and garlic and cook 2 minutes, stirring occasionally. Add the peppers, oregano, thyme, parsley and seasoning and cook gently 2–3 minutes longer until the peppers are soft; keep warm.

Broil the bass, skin side away from the flame at first, for 4–6 minutes on each side, depending on its thickness or until it flakes easily when tested with a fork. Brush the bass from time to time with reserved marinade and turn once.

Arrange the bass, overlapping, down one side of a platter and spoon the garnish down the other side.

Blowfish

These are often called sea squab because the only edible part (along the backbone) looks like a chicken drumstick. Blowfish are good sautéed or deep fried; the center bone is spineless so the fish is very easy to eat.

Bluefish

Common along the Atlantic coast, bluefish have an agreeable flavor. They are best cooked very simply with mild seasonings, as in the following recipe.

Baked Bluefish with Crab Meat

3½–4 lb whole bluefish, cleaned, with head and tail left on
¼ cup butter
salt and pepper
1 cup white wine

For stuffing
2 cups (1 lb) crab meat
1 cup fresh white breadcrumbs
2 teaspoons tarragon
juice of ½ lemon
1 egg, beaten to mix

Method
Combine all ingredients for the stuffing; season well. Set oven at moderate (350°F).

Wash the cavity of the fish, wipe dry with paper towels and fill with stuffing. Lay the fish in a buttered baking dish; with a sharp knife, score the top diagonally every 2 inches so the fish cooks evenly.

Dot the top with butter, sprinkle with salt and pepper and pour around the wine. Cover with foil and bake in heated oven for 30–40 minutes, basting occasionally, or until the fish flakes easily when tested with a fork. Serve with baked tomatoes.

Baked Tomatoes

4–6 ripe tomatoes
black pepper, freshly ground
3 tablespoons grated Parmesan cheese
2 tablespoons browned breadcrumbs
¼ cup melted butter

Method
Cut the cores from the tomatoes, halve them crosswise and scoop out some of the seeds. Sprinkle them with

pepper and set in a buttered baking dish. Set oven at moderate (350°F).

Combine the cheese, breadcrumbs and melted butter and spread the mixture on the tomatoes. Bake in heated oven for 15 minutes or until they are very hot but still firm.

Butterfish

As their name implies, butterfish have soft, tender flesh. They are very small, sometimes weighing only $\frac{1}{4}$ lb, so 3–4 are needed for 1 serving. They must be cooked quickly — either broiled for 2–3 minutes on each side or sautéed briskly in butter. Serve them with lemon wedges and a savory butter like anchovy or maître d'hôtel (see page 55).

Carp

These freshwater fish are valued for their plump flesh in countries as far apart as China and Israel. In medieval Europe every monastery had its carp pond, and carp is still popular today.

Unfortunately the flavor can be flat, due to the carp's habit of burrowing in mud. They have spiny fins and huge scales, so are a nuisance to prepare. However, when baked with plenty of seasoning as in the recipes popular in Eastern Europe, carp can be excellent, particularly smaller fish weighing up to 7 lb.

Polish Carp with Beer

4–5 whole carp, cleaned, with head and tail left on
1 cup beer
$\frac{1}{2}$ teaspoon salt
$\frac{1}{4}$ teaspoon black pepper, freshly ground
$\frac{1}{2}$ teaspoon ground cloves
grated rind of $\frac{1}{2}$ lemon
1 large onion, chopped
2 tablespoons butter
2 tablespoons vinegar
$\frac{1}{4}$ cup golden raisins

Method
Wash the carp, trim the fins, and scrape off the scales. Slash the top of the carp deeply with diagonal cuts 2 inches apart and rub the fish with salt, pepper, cloves and grated lemon rind. Set oven at moderate (350°F).

In a shallow flameproof casserole or roasting pan fry the onion in butter until golden brown. Lay the fish on top, pour over the beer and vinegar, sprinkle over the raisins and cover the fish loosely with foil.

Bake in heated oven for 30–40 minutes or until the fish flakes easily when tested with a fork. Serve with braised red cabbage.

Catfish

Catfish have feelers that look like a cat's whiskers and they are found in freshwater streams and rivers throughout North America.

There are several varieties; they are sold whole or in fillets and must be skinned before cooking. A favorite way to cook them is to coat them with flour, egg and cornmeal instead of breadcrumbs and then shallow fry them in bacon fat or deep fry them in oil.

Cod, Haddock, Hake (Ling) and Pollack

All these white fleshed fish are among the many varieties that are found on northern Atlantic fishing grounds. Cod and haddock were discussed in Volume 2.

Frogs' Legs

Frogs' legs are only available frozen, except in production areas where they may be sold fresh at local fish markets. They come skinned in pairs ready to cook and the smallest ones are the best — $\frac{3}{4}$ lb frogs' legs makes 1 generous serving. Frogs legs taste like delicate, tender chicken and the same flavorings as for chicken — wine, herbs, cream, tomatoes, mushrooms — are good with them.

Frogs' Legs Poulette

12–14 pairs (3 lb) frogs' legs (depending on size)
1 cup white wine
2 tablespoons butter
1 shallot, finely chopped
1 tablespoon flour
$\frac{1}{2}$ cup chicken stock
2 egg yolks
$\frac{1}{2}$ cup heavy cream
1 tablespoon chopped parsley
salt and pepper

Method
Soak the frogs' legs in cold water for 1–2 hours, drain and dry on paper towels. Boil the wine until reduced by half.

In a shallow flameproof casserole heat the butter and brown the frogs' legs quickly on both sides. Take out, add the shallot and cook gently until soft. Stir in the flour, cook until it is straw-colored and pour in the wine and stock. Bring to a boil, stirring, put back the frogs' legs, cover and simmer gently for 10–15 minutes or until they are very tender. Drain the frogs' legs, transfer them to a serving dish and keep warm.

Mix the egg yolks with the cream and add a little of the hot sauce; stir this liaison into the remaining sauce. Heat gently, stirring until it thickens slightly.

Watchpoint: do not boil the sauce or it will curdle.

Take the sauce from the heat, stir in the parsley and adjust the seasoning. Spoon the sauce over the frogs' legs; serve with boiled rice or baby lima beans.

Flounder Dieppoise is garnished with mussels and shrimps and browned before serving

Flounder

The merits of flounder often pass unrecognized because they are mistakenly called sole. Lemon and grey sole are really members of the flounder family.

Flounder are excellent flatfish with a sweet delicate flavor, although lacking the firm texture characteristic of European sole. Flounder are sold whole or in fillets and the smaller the fish, the better the flavor. Black-backed flounder are a popular variety here, and there are many other varieties.

You can cook flounder almost any way you like and they are particularly good served with a rich wine or butter sauce.

Maître d'Hôtel Butter

Cream $\frac{1}{4}$ cup butter on a plate with a metal spatula, then work in 2 teaspoons chopped parsley, a few drops of lemon juice and salt and pepper to taste.

Flounder Colbert

4 whole flounder ($\frac{3}{4}$ to 1 lb each) skinned, with heads and tails left on

For coating
$\frac{1}{2}$ cup seasoned flour (made with $\frac{1}{2}$ teaspoon salt, $\frac{1}{4}$ teaspoon pepper)
1 egg, beaten to mix
$\frac{1}{2}$–$\frac{3}{4}$ cup dry white breadcrumbs
deep fat (for frying)

For serving
$\frac{1}{4}$ cup maître d'hôtel butter
1 lemon, cut in wedges

The dish is named for **Jean-Baptiste Colbert**, a statesman and patron of the arts in the reign of Louis XIV.

Method

With a small sharp knife make a cut right down the center of each flounder, along the backbone on the side that had white skin (side with thinner fillets). With short, sharp strokes, detach the fillets from the bone, working from the center, but leave them attached at the top and bottom and at the outside edges. Trim the sides with scissors and square off the tails.

Wash the fish and dry them on paper towels. Coat them well with seasoned flour, brush with beaten egg and coat with breadcrumbs, pressing them in firmly, including the insides of loosened fillets. Roll the loosened fillets outwards, exposing the backbone.

Heat deep fat to 375°F on a fat thermometer. Gently lower in the fish, 1–2 at a time, depending on the size of the pan, and fry 5–6 minutes until golden brown. Push them under the surface of the fat with a slotted spatula so they brown on top as well as underneath. Drain them well on paper towels.

With scissors snip the backbone of the fish at the head and tail, cut it in sections and pull it out. Arrange the fish on a platter and reheat in a moderate oven (350°F) for 1–2 minutes.

Place a strip of chilled maître d'hôtel butter in the center of each fish (between the rolled back fillets) and serve with lemon wedges.

Flounder Dieppoise

1$\frac{1}{2}$–2 lb flounder fillets
juice of $\frac{1}{2}$ lemon
3 pints fresh mussels or 1 can (9 oz) mussels, drained
1 onion, quartered
1 cup white wine
$\frac{1}{2}$ cup water
1 cup ($\frac{1}{2}$ lb) cooked, peeled baby shrimps
2 tablespoons grated Parmesan cheese

For sauce
3 tablespoons butter
2 tablespoons flour
1$\frac{1}{2}$ cups liquid from mussels
$\frac{1}{2}$ cup light cream
salt and pepper

Method

Set oven at moderate (350°F).

Wash and dry the flounder fillets. Cut them in half down the center and fold under the ends neatly. Lay them in a buttered baking dish, sprinkle with lemon juice and cover with buttered foil. Bake in heated oven for 10–12 minutes or until fish flakes when tested with a fork.

To prepare fresh mussels: scrub them well, discarding any that are open and do not close when tapped. Put them in a kettle with the onion, wine and water, cover and bring to a boil, shaking the pan occasionally. Cook 2 minutes or until the mussels open, then remove them from their shells, discarding the beard (the gristle around the shell). Discard any mussels that do not open. Reserve the mussels, strain the liquid and measure 1$\frac{1}{2}$ cups.

If using canned mussels: drain them and reserve the liquid. Simmer the mussel liquid with the onion, wine and water in a covered pan for 10 minutes or until reduced to 1$\frac{1}{2}$ cups; strain.

To make the sauce: in a saucepan melt the butter, stir in the flour off the heat and add the mussel liquid. Bring to a boil, stirring, and simmer 2 minutes. Add the cream, bring just back to a boil and taste for seasoning.

Arrange the fillets in a serving dish, scatter with mussels and shrimps and coat with sauce. Sprinkle with cheese and brown under the broiler before serving.

Fillets of Flounder Dugléré

1½–2 lb flounder fillets
1½ cups fish stock

For sauce
2 tomatoes, peeled, seeded and cut in strips
1 tablespoon chopped parsley
3 tablespoons butter
2½ tablespoons flour
stock (from cooking fish)
½ cup light cream
salt and pepper

If you want to avoid making fish stock for poaching the flounder, pour ¾ cup water and ¾ cup bottled clam juice over the fish, add 1–2 slices of onion, cover with buttered foil and cook as below. Then drain fish and strain stock into sauce.

Method
Set oven at moderate (350°F).
Wash and dry the fillets, cut them in half lengthwise and fold them, skinned side under and tail end on top. Lay them in a buttered baking dish and pour over the stock. Cover with buttered foil and poach in heated oven for 10–12 minutes or until the fish just flakes easily when tested with a fork. Cool slightly, then drain, reserving the stock, and keep warm on a platter.
To prepare the sauce: in a saucepan melt the butter, stir in the flour, cook until straw-colored, then strain in the reserved stock, off the heat. Bring to a boil, stirring, add the cream and seasoning and simmer 2 minutes. Add the tomatoes and parsley, heat thoroughly and spoon over the fish.

Fish cooked in **Dugléré** style always means with a velouté sauce with tomatoes and parsley. It is named for the French chef Dugléré who used to work at the famous Café Anglais in Paris (the Café no longer exists).

Fish Stock
Peel and slice 1 large onion, blanch, drain and refresh it. Melt 1 tablespoon butter in a large saucepan, add the onion and 1 lb washed fish bones, cover and cook slowly for 5 minutes. Add 1 carrot, peeled and sliced, 1 stalk of celery, sliced, 5 cups water, bouquet garni, ½ teaspoon salt, 6 peppercorns, ½ cup dry white wine and a slice of lemon. Simmer gently, uncovered, for 20 minutes; strain and measure.

Grouper

These saltwater fish are known for their gift of camouflage. The most abundant variety, Red Grouper, is usually found at sea bottom or hidden in seaweed and coral in the warm waters from Virginia to Brazil.
Their usual market size is from 5–15 lb, but they can grow as large as 40 lb. Groupers are sold whole or in fillets. They can be substituted in any recipe using sea bass or red snapper.

Halibut

These are excellent flat fish with a firm texture and superb flavor. Halibut are huge fish, sometimes weighing up to 600 lb, although the average weight is usually about 50 lb. A chicken halibut of up to 10 lb is delicious if you can find it; larger halibut are usually sold in steaks.

Halibut with Mushrooms and Shrimps

1½–2 lb halibut steaks
1 cup (¼ lb) mushrooms, sliced
¾ cup white wine, or fish stock
salt and pepper
3–4 tomatoes, peeled and sliced
1 tablespoon butter
1 tablespoon chopped parsley (for sprinkling)

For sauce
½ cup (¼ lb) cooked, peeled shrimps, chopped
1 shallot, finely chopped
2 tablespoons butter
1½ tablespoons flour
1½ cups milk
2 tablespoons heavy cream

Method
Set oven at moderate (350°F).
Arrange the halibut steaks in a buttered baking dish and scatter the mushrooms on top. Pour over the wine or stock, season and cover with buttered foil. Poach in heated oven for 12–15 minutes or until the fish flakes easily when tested with a fork.
Place the tomato slices, overlapping, down the center of another baking dish (the fish will be served in this), dot with butter and cover with buttered foil. Bake in oven with the fish for 5–7 minutes.
Lift out the fish steaks, reserving the cooking liquid, drain them on paper towels and remove any skin and the central bone, leaving the fish as unbroken as possible with the mushrooms on top. Transfer the fish carefully onto the tomatoes and keep warm.
To make the sauce: strain the cooking liquid from the fish into a pan, add the shallot and boil to reduce to 2–3 tablespoons. In a saucepan melt the butter, stir in the flour off the heat and pour in the milk. Bring to a boil, stirring, season and simmer 5 minutes or until it is slightly reduced.
Add the shallot mixture and bring the sauce back to a boil. Stir in the shrimps and cream, heat well, taste for seasoning and spoon the sauce over the fish. Sprinkle with chopped parsley and serve.

Kingfish

Kingfish, called king mackerel, are caught off the Florida and Pacific coast. They are a fierce game fish, weighing up to 75 lb. The flesh is dark, with a good flavor and there are few bones — cook them like bass.

Mullet

There are many kinds of mullet, often named according to their color. They are small fish, usually 2–3 lb, firm-fleshed, with a sweet delicate taste. For fish of this size, cook as for red snapper.
When you can find them, buy baby mullet of about 1 lb, each serving 1 person, and broil or bake them with a duxelles stuffing. They are also delicious cooked 'en papillote' — in a paper or foil case.

Mullet en Papillote

4 mullet (¾–1 lb each),
   cleaned, heads and tails left
   on
¼ cup butter
salt
black pepper, freshly ground
juice of ½ lemon
4–6 tablespoons melted butter
   (for serving)

This recipe is excellent if a mushroom duxelles mixture is spread on the mullet before baking.

Method

Wash the fish and dry well. Set oven at moderate (350°F).

Cut 4 ovals of silicone paper or foil large enough to enclose each fish. Spread the center of each paper generously with butter, place a fish on top and season well, adding a squeeze of lemon juice. Fold the paper over the fish, turn over the edges and pleat them so they are sealed.

Set the packages on a baking sheet and bake in the heated oven for 15–18 minutes—if using silicone paper it should become puffed and brown.

Serve the fish on individual plates, leaving each guest to open his package. Serve melted butter separately.

For mullet 'en papillote,' first place fish on buttered silicone paper and add the lemon juice

Fold and pleat edges of paper case to seal well so fish juices do not escape during cooking

Pike

A freshwater fish with a ferocious reputation for attacking others, pike vary in size—monsters up to 60 lb have been landed.

The flesh has a good flavor and a characteristic close texture that makes it an ideal base for savory molds made with pounded raw fish. The classic French dish, quenelles (light smooth dumplings made of fish), are best made with pike (a recipe will be given in a future Volume).

Pike are also good baked or braised à la Bourguignonne (see recipe for braised fish in Volume 5).

Mushroom Duxelles

In a skillet cook 1 shallot or scallion, finely chopped, in 2 tablespoons butter until soft. Add 2 cups (½ lb) mushrooms, finely chopped, and cook over brisk heat for 2–3 minutes, stirring, until all the moisture has evaporated.

Stir in 2 tablespoons chopped parsley and salt and pepper to taste.

Pompano in white wine is served with a border of browned mashed potato

Pompano

Most pompano come from Florida; they are small fish, so are ideal for stuffing to serve whole, and are also available in fillets. A favorite way of serving is 'en papillote', like mullet, and they are often filled with a crab meat stuffing before baking.

The rich creamy flesh is a gourmet delicacy, but pompano are expensive as supplies are limited.

Pompano in White Wine

1½ lb pompano fillets
juice of 1 lemon
salt and pepper
3 medium potatoes, boiled and mashed with ¼ cup hot milk, 2 tablespoons butter, and salt and pepper
1–2 tablespoons chopped parsley

For white wine sauce
½ cup white wine
1 shallot, finely chopped
6 peppercorns
blade of mace
1 egg yolk, lightly beaten
½ cup butter
2 tablespoons flour
1½ cups fish stock

Method
Wash and dry the fish; fold the fillets in half if they are small or cut them in serving pieces if they are large.

Place them in a buttered baking dish, add a squeeze of lemon juice, season and cover with buttered foil. Bake in a moderate oven (350°F) for 12–15 minutes or until the fish flakes easily when tested with a fork.

To make the white wine sauce: put the wine, shallot,

peppercorns and mace in a pan and boil until reduced to 2 teaspoons. With a wooden spoon beat the egg yolk in a small bowl with ½ tablespoon butter until light and slightly thick. Strain on the wine, set the bowl over a pan of boiling water, turn off the heat and add 5 tablespoons butter in small pieces, stirring vigorously all the time. When the sauce is light and thick, cover and reserve.

To finish the white wine sauce: make a roux by melting remaining 2 tablespoons butter, stir in the flour and cook, stirring, until a pale-straw color. Cool slightly, pour in the fish stock and bring the sauce to a boil, stirring. Simmer 5 minutes or until the sauce is well-flavored and the consistency of heavy cream; taste for seasoning and cool slightly. Beat reserved butter sauce, a little at a time, into the fish sauce, off the heat, and keep hot in a water bath.

Drain the fish fillets on paper towels and arrange them in a serving dish. Spoon the wine sauce over the fish. Pipe a border of mashed potato around the edge of the dish and brown under the broiler. Sprinkle with chopped parsley and serve.

Pompano Stuffed with Shellfish

4 small pompano (about 1 lb each)
¼ cup melted butter
3 tablespoons fresh white breadcrumbs
salt and pepper
bunch of watercress (for garnish)

For filling
1 cup (¼ lb) mushrooms, sliced
2 tablespoons butter
1½ tablespoons flour
1 cup milk
½ lb crab meat or cooked, peeled chopped shrimps
1 tablespoon heavy cream

Method
Have the fish skinned on both sides, but with the heads left on. Trim the tails and then wash the fish well. With a sharp knife make a cut along the center back of the fish and cut down one side of the backbone and open up the back.

Brush a baking sheet with melted butter and lay the fish

on it, belly down. Set the oven at moderately hot (375°F).

To prepare the filling: sauté the mushrooms in a pan in half the butter for 1–2 minutes until soft. Take from the heat, add the remaining butter and stir in the flour off the heat. Blend in the milk and bring to a boil, stirring. Simmer 2 minutes, take from the heat, add the crab meat or shrimps and cream and season well.

Put this mixture into the slit along the back of the fish. Brush the fish and stuffing with melted butter, sprinkle with breadcrumbs and a little seasoning, and bake in heated oven for 15–20 minutes or until the fish flakes easily when tested with a fork.

With a spatula transfer the fish carefully on to a platter and garnish with watercress.

Porgy (or Scup)

These are a popular game fish and many varieties are found all along the Atlantic coast. They are usually sold whole; sauté them in butter and serve with broiled tomatoes.

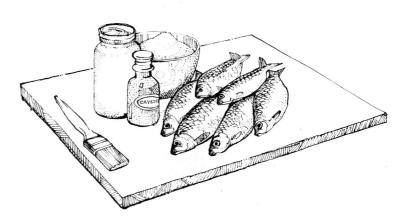

Red Snapper

One of the most popular gourmet fishes in North America, red snapper look as good as they taste. They come from the Caribbean and South Atlantic and, with their pink skin, they make a spectacular dish when baked whole and served, hot or cold, with a colorful garnish, or contrasting sauce like genevoise (see trout recipe, page 65) or a green or tomato mayonnaise.

Red snapper are usually sold in fillets or steaks but small portion size ones are available as well as ones of 5 lb or more.

Poached Red Snapper

5–6 lb whole red snapper, cleaned, head and tail left on
court bouillon (made with 2 quarts water, 1 sliced carrot, 1 sliced onion stuck with 1 clove, bouquet garni, 12 peppercorns, $\frac{1}{4}$ cup vinegar or lemon juice and 1 teaspoon salt)

Both sea and striped bass and salmon are also excellent poached in this manner.

Method
Wash the snapper, dry it thoroughly, trim the fins and tail and set it in a fish kettle. If this is not available, wrap the snapper in cheesecloth, leaving a length of cloth at each end so the fish can be lifted easily, and lay it in a baking dish or roasting pan. Pour over the court bouillon – it should cover the fish. Cover the kettle and simmer on top of the stove or poach in a moderate oven (350°F) for 20–25 minutes or until the fish flakes easily when tested with a fork.

To serve hot: lift the fish from the hot court bouillon, remove the cheesecloth, if used, and set the fish on a white linen napkin on a large platter. (The napkin absorbs any liquid.) Decorate the top with overlapping slices of lemon and serve the snapper with hollandaise or genevoise sauce and cucumber salad.

To serve cold: leave snapper in the court bouillon until cool, then lift it out, drain thoroughly and set on a platter. Decorate the top of the fish with overlapping slices of unpeeled cucumber and garnish the platter with watercress and tomato baskets filled with peeled, diced cucumber. Serve with green or tomato mayonnaise.

Green Mayonnaise
Into $1\frac{1}{2}$ cups mayonnaise stir 2 tablespoons finely chopped parsley, 1 tablespoon finely chopped chives, 1 tablespoon finely chopped tarragon and 1 teaspoon finely chopped dill. Alternatively, purée the herbs with mayonnaise in a blender. Cover mayonnaise and let stand in a cool place at least 2 hours for the flavor to mellow before serving.

Tomato Mayonnaise
To $1\frac{1}{2}$ cups mayonnaise add 1 tablespoon tomato paste or to taste, so that mayonnaise is well colored and flavored.

Red Snapper Niçoise

5–6 lb red snapper, trimmed and head removed, or $1\frac{1}{2}$–2 lb red snapper fillets
$\frac{1}{4}$ cup olive oil
2 cloves of garlic, chopped
2 teaspoons paprika
1 tablespoon tomato paste
1 teaspoon thyme
salt
black pepper, freshly ground
1 cup white wine or tomato juice
$\frac{1}{2}$ cup pitted Italian-type ripe olives
lemon wedges (for garnish)

Method
Set oven at moderate (350°F).

In a small pan heat the oil, add the garlic and sauté gently for 1 minute. Take from heat and stir in the paprika, tomato paste, thyme, salt and pepper and wine or tomato juice; mix well, bring to a boil and simmer 2–3 minutes.

Lay the snapper in a baking dish and, if the fish is whole, score the top deeply in diagonal slashes 2 inches apart. Spoon over the sauce and bake in heated oven for 35–40 minutes for a whole fish, or 15–20 minutes for fillets, or until the fish flakes easily when tested with a fork. Baste from time to time and add the olives 10 minutes before the end of cooking.

Serve the snapper hot or cold, garnished with wedges of lemon.

Sole

The European sole, popularly known as English, Channel or Dover sole, are highly prized for their firm texture and superb flavor; they are not found in American waters, although small quantities are imported frozen.

Several kinds of fish are known as sole in North America but like English sole they are in fact almost always members of the flounder family.

This does not mean that the classic French recipes for sole need be ignored – flounder is an excellent substitute for sole, especially when it is small and freshly caught.

Sole Meunière aux Moules
(Sole with Mussels)

$1\frac{1}{2}$ lb sole fillets
1 quart fresh mussels or 1 can (9 oz) mussels, drained
$\frac{1}{2}$ cup unsalted butter
$\frac{1}{4}$ cup seasoned flour (made with $\frac{1}{4}$ teaspoon salt and pinch of pepper)
juice and grated rind of $\frac{1}{2}$ lemon
1 tablespoon chopped parsley
black pepper, freshly ground
1 lemon, cut in wedges (for serving) – optional

For cooking mussels (optional)
bouquet garni
1 stalk of celery
$\frac{1}{2}$ cup water

Method
To prepare fresh mussels: scrub them well, discarding any that do not close when tapped. Put them in a kettle with the bouquet garni and celery. Add the water, cover the pan and cook over high

Sole with mussels – the fish fillets are fried and served with the mussels and their sauce poured over

heat for 5 minutes or until the mussels open, stirring once. Remove them from their shells, discarding the beard (the gristle around the shell). Discard any mussels that do not open. Melt 2 tablespoons butter, add fresh or canned mussels and keep warm.

Coat the fillets in the seasoned flour. In a large frying pan or skillet heat 3 tablespoons of butter. When it starts to foam, put in the fillets, skinned side up. Fry 2–3 minutes on each side until fillets are golden brown. Drain well on paper towels.

Arrange the fillets, overlapping, down the center of a platter and keep warm.

Wipe out the frying pan or skillet, add the remaining butter and the lemon rind and cook gently to a light brown. At once add the lemon juice, mussels, chopped parsley and pepper, shake over the heat for a few seconds and pour over the sole. Serve the fish hot with lemon wedges arranged around the dish or passed separately.

For sole with mussels, fry the fish fillets in butter until golden brown

Pour the butter, lemon juice, mussels and parsley mixture over fillets of sole

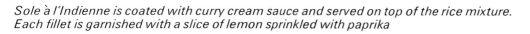
Sole à l'Indienne is coated with curry cream sauce and served on top of the rice mixture.
Each fillet is garnished with a slice of lemon sprinkled with paprika

Sole à l'Indienne

1½–2 lb sole fillets
salt
6 peppercorns
juice of ½ lemon
1 lemon, sliced (for garnish)
paprika (for garnish)

For curry cream sauce
2 teaspoons curry powder
1 tablespoon oil
½ onion, finely chopped
1 clove of garlic, chopped
1¼ cups tomato juice
pepper
2–3 slices of lemon
1 tablespoon apricot jam
1½ cups mayonnaise

For rice mixture
¾ cup rice
1 cup (¼ lb) mushrooms, sliced
squeeze of lemon juice
½ lb cooked, peeled small shrimps
6 tablespoons vinaigrette dressing

If preparing this dish ahead of time, set the fillets on the rice mixture but do not coat with sauce. Cover platter and keep in refrigerator for up to 4 hours. Coat with sauce and garnish just before serving.

Method

Set oven at moderate (350°F).

Wash and dry the fillets and divide them in half down the center. Fold in half crosswise and place in a buttered baking dish; season with a little salt, lay peppercorns on one side of the dish and squeeze over the lemon juice. Cover with buttered foil and bake in heated oven for 10–12 minutes or until the fish flakes easily when tested with a fork. Cool the fish and drain well on paper towels.

To make curry cream sauce: heat the oil and fry the onion and garlic gently until soft.

Stir in the curry powder and cook 2 minutes, then add tomato juice. Simmer 7–10 minutes, then add salt and pepper and lemon slices. Stir in the jam and strain the sauce. Cool it slightly, then beat enough into the mayonnaise to thin it to a coating consistency. Taste for seasoning — it should be well seasoned and lightly colored with tomato.

To make the rice mixture: cook the rice in boiling salted water for 10–12 minutes or until just tender, drain, refresh and drain again. Spread out on a tray or platter and dry in a warm place for 10–15 minutes.

Cook the mushrooms in a heavy pan over low heat with seasoning and a squeeze of lemon juice until soft; cool them. Mix the rice, mushrooms and shrimps with vinaigrette dressing and spoon down the center of a platter.

Arrange the fillets, overlapping slightly, on top of the rice and coat them with curry cream sauce. Top each fillet with a slice of lemon sprinkled with paprika and serve the remaining curry cream sauce separately.

Squid

Fresh squid are available in many large city fish markets all year. They look like baby octopus with 10 legs, and both legs and body are edible.

To clean squid, slit open the belly and remove the bone. Near this is a sac of dark 'ink' that can be used when squid is cooked in a sauce. Remove the sac, then rinse the squid thoroughly.

Squid can be deep or shallow fried or cooked in a sauce — do not overcook or they become tough and rubbery.

Squid with Anchovy

4–6 small squid
3–4 anchovy fillets, soaked in milk to remove excess salt
small piece of dried hot red pepper
bouquet garni
½ cup olive oil
1 onion, finely sliced
1 clove of garlic, crushed
1 cup white wine
½ cup water
black pepper, freshly ground
salt

Method

Remove the bone and ink sac from the squid and wash them well. Cut in 1 inch pieces.

Drain and chop anchovies; tie the red pepper with the bouquet garni.

In a skillet or shallow flameproof casserole, heat the oil and cook the onion with the garlic until soft. Add the wine, water and anchovy, bouquet garni and black pepper.

Add the squid meat, cover and simmer gently until the squid is tender; cooking time — anywhere from 20 minutes to 1 hour — depends entirely on

the age of the squid. Do not overcook or the squid will toughen.

Taste for seasoning, remove the bouquet garni and pepper tied together and serve the squid with boiled rice.

Squid with Tomatoes

4–6 small squid
¼ cup olive oil
3 onions, sliced
2 tomatoes, peeled, seeded and chopped
1 tablespoon tomato paste
3 cloves of garlic, crushed
½ teaspoon oregano
½ teaspoon thyme
1 cup red wine
1 cup water
salt and pepper

Method

To clean the squid: slit open the belly and remove the bone. Immerse the squid in warm water and pull off the purplish outer skin. Remove the sac of dark ink from near the bone; rinse the squid thoroughly. Cut the tentacles into 1 inch pieces and the body into rings.

In a large skillet or shallow flameproof casserole, heat the oil and fry the onions until they are browned. Add the tomatoes, tomato paste, garlic, oregano and thyme, cover and cook gently for 5 minutes. Add the wine and simmer, uncovered, for 5 minutes. Add the water and seasoning, cover and cook gently for 1½ hours or until the squid rings are tender.
Watchpoint: do not let the squid boil or the pieces will become very tough and rubbery. Also, do not overcook.

The mixture should be thick; if not, remove the lid towards the end of cooking so the liquid evaporates. Taste for seasoning and serve with boiled rice.

Trout

Trout are a superb close-textured fish with a sweet nutty flavor. Most varieties live in fresh water although some migrate, like salmon, between salt and fresh water. Trout are widely available fresh and frozen.

Most trout are small so that 1 is served for each person, but a few varieties like salmon trout can be as large as 2½–3 lb.

Cook trout as simply as possible – pan fried in butter or poached and served with a sauce. More trout recipes will be given in a future Volume.

Smoked Trout Pâté

3 smoked trout
salt
black pepper, freshly ground
juice of ½ lemon
2 tablespoons white wine
½ lb haddock or flounder fillet
½ cup fresh white breadcrumbs
1 egg yolk
2 tablespoons butter
1–2 tablespoons heavy cream
1–2 bay leaves
½ cup melted butter

1 terrine or bowl (1 quart capacity) or 4 individual ovenproof dishes with lids

Method
Remove the heads, tails, skin and bones from the trout and discard; cut the flesh of 2 into finger-length pieces and place in a bowl. Sprinkle with salt, pepper, and lemon juice, pour over the wine and leave the fish in the marinade for about 2 hours, turning from time to time.

Set the oven at moderately low (325°F).

Grind or pound the haddock or flounder fillet with the remaining whole trout and add the breadcrumbs, egg yolk, butter and cream.

Strain the marinade from the pieces of trout into the haddock mixture and season to taste.

Cover the bottom of the terrine or bowl or the dishes with a layer of this mixture, add a layer of trout pieces and continue until all the ingredients are used, ending with a layer of breadcrumbs and fish mixture.

Put ½ bay leaf on top of the small dishes or 1 bay leaf on the terrine or bowl, cover with foil, add the lid(s) and bake in a water bath in heated oven for about 45 minutes for the large terrine or bowl, or 20–25 minutes for the individual dishes, or until a skewer inserted in the center for 1 minute is hot to the touch when removed. Let pâté cool.

Remove the lid(s) and foil and cover the pâté with wax paper; put a 2 lb weight on top or ½–1 lb weights on individual dishes and chill overnight. Remove bay leaves and pour a little melted butter over the pâté to seal. It will keep, unopened, for 3–4 days in the refrigerator.

Turn out the large pâté or leave the small ones in the dishes. Serve with hot toast and unsalted butter.

Trout à la Genevoise

4 trout (¾–1 lb each) cleaned, with heads and tails left on
½ cup water
5 peppercorns
salt
'fish' potatoes (for garnish)

For sauce
1 small onion, finely chopped
1 small carrot, finely chopped
2 tablespoons butter
1 cup red wine
kneaded butter, made with
  2 tablespoons butter,
  1 tablespoon flour
¼ teaspoon anchovy paste
¼ teaspoon thyme
1 tablespoon chopped parsley
pepper

Method
Set oven at moderate (350°F).

Trim the fins of the trout, cut the tails in a 'V' and wash and dry the fish. Lay the trout in a buttered baking dish and add the water and peppercorns with a little salt. Cover with buttered foil and poach in heated oven for about 15 minutes or until the fish flakes easily when tested with a fork. Transfer the trout to a platter and keep warm. Strain the cooking liquid and reserve.

To make the sauce: sauté the onion and carrot in 1 tablespoon butter for 2 minutes or until the butter is absorbed. Add the wine and boil until it is reduced by half. Add the reserved fish liquid and simmer 4–5 minutes. Thicken the sauce with kneaded butter, whisking in a few pieces at a time until the sauce is the consistency of heavy cream.

Add the anchovy paste, thyme, parsley, salt and pepper. Whisk in the remaining butter, piece by piece, off the heat; spoon the sauce over trout. Garnish the platter with 'fish' potatoes and serve.

Add the reserved fish liquid to the reduced red wine mixture

'Fish' Potatoes

These are shaped from large white potatoes and are so named because they frequently accompany fish dishes.

Choose 3–4 medium-sized potatoes, peel and quarter them lengthwise. Pare away the sharp edges with a peeler and shape them into ovals. Boil in a pan of salted water for about 7 minutes, drain and return them to the pan.

Cover with foil and the pan lid and continue cooking 4–5 minutes over a very low heat or until tender.

This method prevents the potatoes from breaking and makes them dry and floury.

Trout à la Genevoise, served with a red wine sauce, is garnished with 'fish' potatoes (recipe is on page 65)

Fresh Tuna

Game fish found on both coasts, fresh tuna are sold whole, in steaks or fillets. Albacore tuna — all white meat that is usually canned — is the best. Poach tuna as for red snapper (see page 60) and serve cold with mayonnaise or Béarnaise sauce.

Whitefish

These are freshwater fish from the Great Lakes and other cold water lakes in North America; supplies are abundant. They weigh from 2–6 lb and come whole or in fillets. The rich flesh is excellent for broiling or poaching or baking with a herb or duxelles stuffing.

Whitefish Florentine

1½–2 lb whitefish fillets
salt
squeeze of lemon juice
1 lb fresh spinach or 2 packages frozen spinach
1 tablespoon butter

For mornay sauce
1½ tablespoons butter
1½ tablespoons flour
1¼ cups milk
¼ cup grated Parmesan or Gruyère cheese
pepper
½ teaspoon prepared or Dijon-style mustard

Method
Set oven at moderate (350°F).
Wash and dry the fillets and cut them in half if they are large, or fold them crosswise if they are small. Lay them in a buttered baking dish and sprinkle with salt and a squeeze of lemon juice. Cover with buttered foil and bake in the heated oven for 10–12 minutes or until fish flakes easily when tested with a fork.

If using fresh spinach, cook it in boiling salted water for 5 minutes or cook frozen spinach according to the package directions. Drain the spinach, refresh and press it between 2 plates to extract all the water. Put spinach back in the pan with the 1 tablespoon butter, toss 1–2 minutes over heat, then arrange it down the center of an ovenproof serving dish. Arrange the fish on top and keep warm.

Make the mornay sauce, reserving half the cheese, and spoon the sauce over the fish. If you like, pipe a duchesse potato border around the dish. Sprinkle reserved cheese on top and brown under the broiler or in a hot oven (425°F). Serve with duchesse potatoes (see Volume 8).

Whiting

These are small round silvery fish with a flaky texture; whiting easily disintegrate if overcooked. One fish per person is the usual serving. Whiting are also sold in fillets.

Whiting Alsacienne

1½–2 lb whiting fillets
1 small head of firm green cabbage, shredded
¼ cup butter
1 onion, finely sliced
salt and pepper
½ cup water
1 bay leaf
1½ tablespoons flour
1 cup milk
¼ cup grated dry Cheddar cheese
1 tablespoon grated Parmesan cheese (for sprinkling)

Method
Melt half the butter in a wide-based flameproof casserole, add the onion, cover and cook 2–3 minutes until soft. Add the cabbage with seasoning, stir to mix, cover and cook slowly for 15–20 minutes, stirring once or twice, or until the cabbage is tender.

Set oven at moderate (350°F).

Wash the fillets, dry and fold them crosswise. Lay them in a buttered baking dish and add the water, bay leaf and seasoning. Cover with buttered foil and poach in heated oven for 10–12 minutes or until the fish flakes easily when tested with a fork. Drain the fish and keep warm; strain the cooking liquid and reserve.

Melt the remaining butter in a saucepan, stir in the flour off the heat and pour in the reserved cooking liquid. Bring to a boil, stirring, and add the milk. Bring back to a boil, simmer 2 minutes, take from the heat and stir in the Cheddar cheese. Adjust the seasoning.

Pile the cabbage down the center of an ovenproof serving dish and arrange the fish on top. Spoon over the sauce, sprinkle Parmesan cheese on top and brown under the broiler or in a hot oven (425°F). Serve with 'fish' potatoes (see page 65).

Moussaka is made with layers of lamb and sliced eggplant, potatoes and tomatoes covered with a rich sauce and sprinkled with grated Parmesan cheese

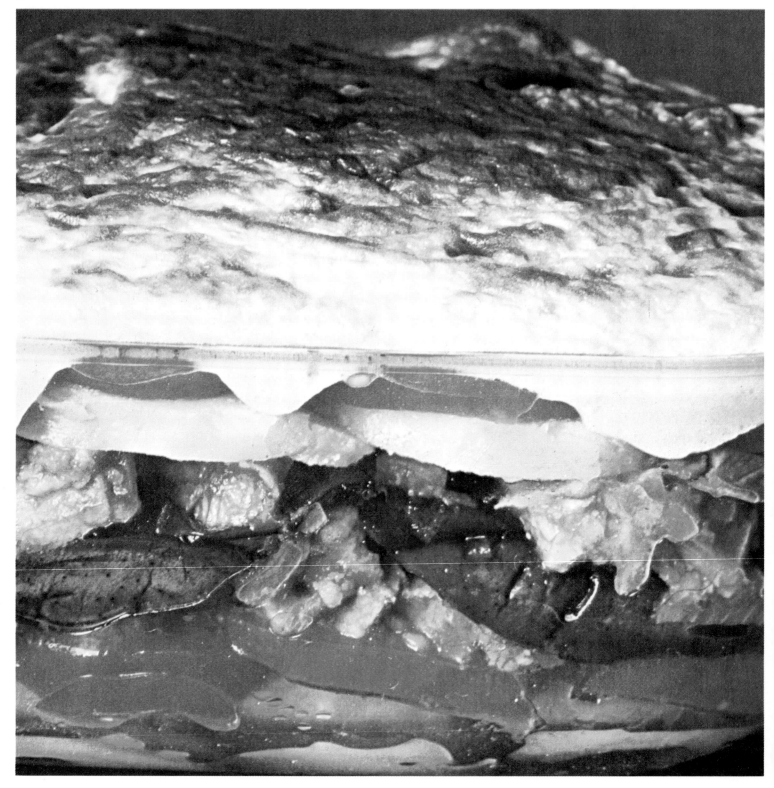

UNUSUAL MEAT DISHES

There are enough meat dishes to serve a different one every day of the month or even, with a little imagination, every day of the year. Many of them, like those that follow, are easy to make and will reheat well.

Moussaka

2–3 cups cooked lamb, cubed
2 medium eggplants
6 tablespoons oil
2 tablespoons butter
2 medium onions,
 finely chopped
½ cup tomato sauce
2 cloves of garlic, crushed
¼ teaspoon ground nutmeg or
 mace
salt and pepper
3–4 potatoes, boiled in their
 skins, peeled and sliced
2–3 tomatoes, peeled, seeded
 and sliced
¼ cup grated Parmesan cheese

For sauce
1½ cups béchamel sauce, made
 with 2 tablespoons butter,
 2 tablespoons flour and
 1½ cups milk (infused with
 slice of onion,
 2–3 peppercorns, blade of
 mace and 2–3 parsley stalks)
½ teaspoon Dijon-style mustard
2 eggs, separated

A recipe for Greek moussaka
is given in Volume 12.

Method
Wipe the eggplants, slice
them, discarding the stem,
sprinkle with salt and leave
30 minutes to draw out juice
(dégorger). Rinse them to
remove excess salt and pat
dry with paper towels.

Brush a baking sheet with
oil, lay the eggplant slices on
it and brush them generously
with oil. Bake in a moderately
hot oven (375°F) for 10
minutes, turn the slices over,
brush them again with oil and
continue baking until they are
brown and tender. Using this
method, the eggplants will
not absorb as much oil as they
would by frying.

In a skillet heat the butter
and fry the onion until soft.
Stir in the meat, tomato
sauce, garlic and nutmeg or
mace with seasoning to taste.

Arrange the meat mixture,
eggplant slices, sliced potatoes and tomatoes in layers in
a buttered baking dish, ending
with potato and tomato.

To make the sauce: beat
mustard and egg yolks into
the béchamel sauce and
season to taste. Whip the egg
whites until they hold a stiff
peak, fold into the sauce and
spoon it over the moussaka.
Sprinkle with grated cheese
and bake in a hot oven (400°F)
for 15 minutes or until
browned.

Dégorger means to re-
move impurities and
strong flavors ' before
cooking. For example,
country ham should be
soaked in cold water for a
specified length of time to
dégorger. Vegetables such
as eggplant or cucumber
should be sprinkled with
salt, covered with a heavy
plate and left up to 1 hour.
Then wash away salt and
press out excess liquid
with a weighted plate or
pat dry with paper towels.

Eggplants Stuffed with Kidneys

2 medium eggplants
4 lambs' kidneys
3 tablespoons butter
2 medium onions, finely sliced
2 teaspoons flour
1 teaspoon tomato paste
¾ cup stock
1 clove of garlic, crushed
1 bay leaf
salt and pepper
2–3 tablespoons oil
2 tomatoes, peeled, seeded
 and chopped
1 tablespoon grated
 Parmesan cheese
1 tablespoon fresh white
 breadcrumbs

Method
Cut the eggplants in half
lengthwise, remove the stems
and run the point of a knife
between the flesh and the
skin. Score the flesh in a
lattice pattern, sprinkle with
salt and let stand 30 minutes
to draw out the juice
(dégorger).

Skin the kidneys, cut out
the cores and cut in half
lengthwise. Heat half the
butter in a skillet, add the
kidneys, cut side down, brown
them on both sides, remove
them and keep warm.

Lower the heat, add remaining butter and the onion and
cook until soft but not
browned. Stir in the flour,
tomato paste and stock and
bring to a boil. Add garlic, bay
leaf and seasoning, put back
kidneys, cover and simmer
about 20 minutes.

Rinse eggplants to remove
excess salt and pat them dry
with paper towels. Heat the
oil in a skillet and sauté the
eggplants gently on both
sides until soft.
Watchpoint: eggplants brown
very quickly, so if the flesh is
brown before they are completely cooked, finish by baking them in a moderate oven
(350°F) until tender.

Scoop out the flesh with a
spoon and chop it, reserving
the eggplant shells. Remove
the bay leaf from the kidneys,
add the tomatoes and egg-
plant flesh and simmer 2–3
minutes.

Set the eggplant shells in a
buttered baking dish, put 2
kidney halves in each and fill
with the rest of the mixture.
Sprinkle the tops with cheese
and breadcrumbs and bake in
a hot oven (425°F) for 7–8
minutes or until brown.

Stuff eggplants with kidneys and tomato to make an excellent supper dish

Beef Galette

2 cups (1 lb) cooked fresh or
   corned beef, ground
4 shallots or 1 medium onion,
   finely chopped
$\frac{1}{2}$ cup butter
1 cup fresh white breadcrumbs
1 tablespoon chopped parsley
4 eggs
$\frac{1}{2}$ cup stock
salt and pepper
5 medium potatoes, peeled
$\frac{1}{4}$ cup hot milk
$\frac{1}{4}$ cup browned breadcrumbs
1–1$\frac{1}{2}$ cups tomato sauce (for
   serving)

*6 inch charlotte mold or 8 inch
   springform pan*

Method
In a skillet fry 2 shallots or half
the onion in $\frac{1}{4}$ cup butter until
soft but not browned. Take
from heat and stir in the
meat, white breadcrumbs and
parsley.

Beat the eggs with the
stock until mixed, pour onto
the meat, add seasoning to
taste and mix well.

Cook potatoes in plenty of
boiling salted water for 15–20
minutes or until tender. Drain
them well and mash with a
potato masher or fork until
smooth.

Melt the remaining butter
in a small pan, fry the remaining shallot or onion until soft
but not browned and add to
the potatoes with the hot
milk. Taste for seasoning and
beat well.

Grease the charlotte mold
or cake pan and sprinkle
thickly with browned crumbs.
Line the bottom and sides of
the mold or pan with the
mashed potato and fill with
meat mixture, pressing it down
well. Cover with foil and bake
in a moderate oven (350°F)
for about 40 minutes or until
firm.

Turn out the galette onto a
hot platter and serve with
tomato sauce.

A **galette** is a round cake
and can refer to almost
any sweet or savory mix-
ture ranging from the
traditional French Twelfth
Night cake made of puff
pastry to the mashed
potato cake filled with
meat given here.

Tomato Sauce

Melt 2 tablespoons butter
in a pan, stir in 1$\frac{1}{2}$ tablespoons flour and blend in
1$\frac{1}{2}$ cups stock or water, off
the heat. Bring to a boil,
stirring.

Take 2 cups of tomatoes
(1 medium can, or 4 fresh
tomatoes), cut in half and
squeeze to remove seeds.
(Peel fresh tomatoes only if
you will be puréeing in a
blender.) Strain the seeds to
remove the juice. Add the
tomatoes and juice to the
sauce with bouquet garni.
Season, add pinch of sugar
and 1 teaspoon tomato paste
to strengthen the flavor, if you
like.

Cover the pan and simmer
gently for 30 minutes or until
the tomatoes are pulpy.
Remove bouquet garni; work
the sauce through a strainer
or purée in a blender. Return
the sauce to the rinsed pan
and adjust seasoning, simmer
5 minutes or until it is the
right consistency.
Note: a tomato sauce should
be of flowing, rather than
coating consistency. For a
good gloss, stir in 1 tablespoon butter before serving.

Beef Olives 1

6 large thin slices (about 1$\frac{1}{2}$ lb)
   round or chuck steak
1 tablespoon oil
1 large onion, sliced
1 large carrot, sliced
1 stalk of celery, sliced
1 tablespoon flour
$\frac{1}{4}$ cup sherry (optional)
2 teaspoons tomato paste
1$\frac{1}{2}$–2 cups stock
salt and pepper
bouquet garni
5 medium potatoes, mashed
   with about $\frac{1}{2}$ cup milk and
   3–4 tablespoons butter

For stuffing
$\frac{1}{2}$ lb ground pork
1 cup ($\frac{1}{2}$ lb) chopped cooked
   ham
1 small onion, finely chopped
2 tablespoons butter
$\frac{1}{4}$ cup fresh white breadcrumbs
2 tablespoons sherry (optional)
1 teaspoon mixed herbs
   (thyme, oregano,
   marjoram)
1 tablespoon chopped parsley
1 small egg

Method
Pound the slices of beef
between 2 sheets of wax
paper, using a rolling pin or
heavy pan. Trim and cut each
slice in half.

To make the stuffing: fry
the onion in the butter until
soft. Add the remaining
ingredients and season well.
Spread the mixture on the
beef slices and roll them up
neatly, then tie with string to
form olive shapes.

In a flameproof casserole
heat the oil and brown beef
rolls all over. Remove them,
add the vegetables, reduce
heat, cover pot and cook
8–10 minutes, stirring occasionally, until the vegetables
are very brown and have
absorbed all the fat. Sprinkle
in the flour and cook 2–3
minutes.

Add the sherry, if used,
bring to a boil, then stir in the
tomato paste and the stock
with seasoning to taste. Put
the beef rolls back into the
casserole, tuck in the bouquet
garni and bring to a boil.
Cover and simmer on top of
the stove or in a moderately
low oven (325°F) for 1$\frac{1}{2}$–2
hours or until tender.

Prepare the mashed pota-
toes and mound them down
the center of a platter. Remove
the strings from the 'olives',
arrange them on the potatoes
and keep warm. Strain the
cooking liquid, boil until
slightly reduced, taste for
seasoning and spoon over the
dish.

Beef Olives 2

6 large thin slices (about 1$\frac{1}{2}$ lb)
   round or chuck steak
1 tablespoon oil
buttered noodles or boiled
   rice (for serving)

For stuffing
1 lb sausage meat
1 shallot
2 tablespoons butter
$\frac{1}{2}$ cup fresh white breadcrumbs
1 tablespoon mixed herbs
   (thyme, rosemary, sage)
1 small egg
salt and pepper

For sauce
$\frac{1}{2}$ lb beef kidney, diced
1 large onion, chopped
2 tablespoons butter
1 tablespoon flour
1$\frac{1}{2}$ teaspoons tomato paste
$\frac{1}{2}$ cup red wine
1 cup beef stock
bouquet garni

This is a richer recipe for beef
olives than the previous one.

Method
Pound and trim the slices of
beef and cut in half as for beef
olives 1.

To make the stuffing: fry the shallot in butter until soft and mix in the remaining ingredients with plenty of seasoning.

Spread the stuffing on the beef slices, roll them up and tie with string to form olive shapes.

In a flameproof casserole heat the oil and brown the beef rolls all over; take them out.

To make the sauce: melt the butter in the oil, add the kidney and onion and fry gently for 5–7 minutes or until browned. Stir in the flour, tomato paste, wine and stock and bring to a boil.

Put back the beef rolls, add bouquet garni, cover and bake in a moderately low oven (325°F) for 1½–2 hours or until very tender. Transfer the beef rolls to a platter, remove the bouquet garni and strings, taste the sauce for seasoning and spoon over the beef 'olives'. Serve with buttered noodles or boiled rice.

The name **beef olives** is given to thin slices of beef that are stuffed and tied in olive-shaped rolls before being cooked slowly in liquid.

American Tamale Pie

3 cups cooked lean pork, cut in small cubes
1 onion, chopped
1 clove of garlic, peeled
3 medium tomatoes, peeled, seeded and chopped
1 tablespoon chili powder
½ teaspoon ground coriander
1 teaspoon oregano
2 tablespoons lard or oil
1 bay leaf
salt
black pepper, freshly ground

For dough
1½ cups yellow cornmeal
½ cup flour
2 teaspoons salt
1½ cups beef stock
2 tablespoons lard or shortening

Casserole (2–3 quart capacity)

Method
To make the dough: sift the cornmeal, flour and salt together. In a large pan heat the stock with the lard or shortening until melted, bring just to a boil, take from the heat and at once beat in the sifted ingredients until the mixture comes away from the sides of the pan. If it is very thick, add a little more stock.

Combine the onion, garlic and tomatoes with chili powder, coriander and oregano and purée in a blender or pound in a mortar and pestle until smooth.

In a skillet melt the lard or oil, add the onion and tomato mixture with the bay leaf and seasoning to taste. Cook, stirring, for 5 minutes. Remove bay leaf.

Line the bottom and sides of the casserole with two-thirds of the dough, pressing it out with your fist. Spread some of the pork on the bottom, add a layer of tomato mixture and continue in layers until all the pork and about two-thirds of the tomato mixture are used.

Pat out the remaining dough between 2 sheets of wax paper and lay it over the pork mixture. Cover the pot and bake in a moderate oven (350°F) for 1 hour or until the dough is firm.

Heat the remaining tomato mixture and serve it separately as a sauce with the pie.

Lasagne with Sausage

¾ lb lasagne
1 lb spiced or mild Italian sausage
1 tablespoon oil
2 onions, sliced
3 cups tomato sauce
2 cloves of garlic, crushed
bouquet garni
1 teaspoon oregano
1 cup stock
salt and pepper

For filling
1 lb ricotta cheese or creamed cottage cheese
1 egg
1 cup grated Parmesan cheese

Method
Brown the sausage on both sides in the oil in a heavy skillet. Add the onion and cook until it is lightly browned. Stir in the tomato sauce, garlic, bouquet garni, oregano, stock and seasoning and bring to a boil. Cover and simmer gently, stirring occasionally, for 1 hour or until the sausage is very tender. Discard the bouquet garni; lift out the sausage and keep warm.

Cook the lasagne in a large pan of simmering salted water for 12–15 minutes or until it is just tender ('al dente'), stirring occasionally to prevent it from sticking. Drain the lasagne, rinse it with hot water and keep in 1–2 cups hot water.

To make the filling: beat the egg into ricotta or cottage cheese, add half the Parmesan cheese and season well.

Butter a shallow baking dish; spoon in a layer of tomato sauce, reserving the sausage. Cover with a layer of lasagne and a layer of cheese filling. Add another layer of lasagne, then sauce mixture and continue until the lasagne, filling and sauce mixture are used, ending with the sauce.

Sprinkle the dish with the remaining Parmesan cheese and bake in a moderate oven (350°F) for 25–30 minutes or until the lasagne is brown and bubbling.

Wrap the sausage in foil and place it to heat in the oven for the last 10 minutes of cooking the lasagne; unwrap it and cut it in diagonal slices; arrange around the edge of the lasagne.

Potage parabère is garnished with strips of carrot, celery and leek (recipe is on page 76)

START AN INFORMAL MENU WITH STEAMING ONION SOUP

Potage Parabère

Braised Breast of Veal with Tomatoes
Gratin Dauphinois

Pears Pralinées
or
Mango Ice

∾

Red wine – Barbaresco (Italy)
or Barbera (California)

Creamy potage parabère starts an informal dinner menu that includes breast of veal stuffed with pork, served with gratin dauphinois of potatoes. For dessert there's a choice of poached pears coated in praline-flavored cream, or a mango ice.

Veal with tomato sauce is hardly ever in better company than with a fine Italian wine. Among the best are those called Barbaresco – smooth, medium-bodied and full of flavor. They hail from northern Italy and, like a good Beaujolais, require relatively little aging – perhaps two years – to be at their best. A fine alternative from California is Barbera, a wine with less finesse, perhaps, but every bit as much fun to drink.

TIMETABLE

Day before
Marinate the veal.
Make and grind praline for pears pralinées.
Pare and poach pears and keep in the syrup.
Prepare and put mango ice in freezer.

Morning
Make soup but do not add liaison; cover and chill.
Cook garnish for soup; cover and chill.
Make stuffing and stuff veal. Braise but do not make sauce. Peel potatoes and keep in cold water. Prepare tomato garnish for veal, ready for cooking.

Assemble equipment for final cooking from 6:40 for dinner around 8 p.m.

Order of Work

6:40
Set oven at moderate (350°F). Slice potatoes and put in oven to cook.

7:10
Put veal in oven to reheat. Coat pears, arrange on platter and chill.

7:30
Cook garnish for veal.

7:40
Turn oven to low to keep gratin Dauphinois warm. Take the veal from the oven, arrange it on platter and keep warm. Make sauce and keep warm. Slice the veal, arrange it on a platter with the garnish, spoon over the sauce, cover and keep warm.

7:50
Reheat the soup without boiling and add the liaison and garnish.

8:00
Serve soup.
Chill coupe for sherbet glasses. Spoon the mango ice into the glasses just before serving.

You will find that **cooking times** given in the individual recipes for these dishes have sometimes been adapted in the timetable to help you when cooking and serving this menu as a party meal.

Some of the ingredients used in making potage parabère

Appetizer

Potage Parabère

4–5 medium onions, thinly sliced
1 tablespoon butter
4 cups veal or chicken stock
salt and pepper
kneaded butter, made with
    4 tablespoons butter,
    2 tablespoons flour
1 tablespoon chopped parsley

For liaison
1 egg yolk
$\frac{1}{3}$ cup light cream

For garnish
1 medium carrot, cut in
    julienne strips
$\frac{1}{2}$ stalk of celery, cut in
    julienne strips
green part of 1 leek, cut in
    julienne strips

Method
Blanch the onions in boiling water for 1 minute, drain thoroughly and return them to the pan with the butter. Cover tightly and cook over low heat until soft but not browned. Pour in the stock, season, bring to a boil and simmer 12–15 minutes or until the onions are very soft.

To make the garnish: cook the prepared vegetables in a little boiling salted water for 6–7 minutes or until tender, drain them thoroughly and keep warm.

Work the onion mixture through a sieve or purée in a blender and return to the pan. Bring to a boil and whisk in the kneaded butter, a few pieces at a time, until the soup is slightly thickened. Simmer 2 minutes.

Mix egg yolk with the cream for liaison, stir in a little hot soup until well blended and stir this mixture back into remaining soup. Heat until the soup thickens.
Watchpoint: do not boil the soup or it will curdle.

Take the soup from the heat and stir in the parsley. Add the drained vegetable garnish to the soup and serve hot.

Entrée

Braised Breast of Veal with Tomatoes

3–3½ lb breast of veal, boned but not rolled (reserve the bones for making stock)
¼ cup butter, or bacon fat
1 medium onion, sliced
1 carrot, sliced
1 stalk of celery, sliced
bouquet garni
2½ cups well-flavored veal stock (made from veal bones, root vegetables and seasoning)
1 tomato, peeled, seeded and chopped or ½ cup tomato purée
salt and pepper
kneaded butter, made with 2 tablespoons butter, 1 tablespoon flour
⅓ cup heavy cream

For marinade
black pepper, freshly ground
pinch of ground mace
grated rind of ½ lemon
squeeze of lemon juice
1 cup white wine

For stuffing
1 onion, chopped
3 tablespoons butter
¾ lb ground pork
1½ cups fresh white breadcrumbs
1 tablespoon mixed herbs (parsley, thyme, marjoram)
1 egg, beaten to mix

For garnish
3–6 medium tomatoes, cut in half
pinch of sugar
6–8 slices of bacon

Method

To marinate the veal: lay it in a shallow dish. Grind over a

Braised breast of veal with tomatoes is carved in slices for serving and garnished with halved cooked tomatoes and bacon

little black pepper and sprinkle with mace. Sprinkle lemon rind over veal, add lemon juice and white wine, cover and let stand in the refrigerator overnight to marinate, turning the meat occasionally.

Set oven at moderate (350°F).

To prepare the stuffing: cook the chopped onion in the butter until soft. Stir into the ground pork with the breadcrumbs, herbs and seasoning, then stir in the beaten egg to bind the mixture.

Remove the veal from the marinade, pat it dry with paper towels and spread the stuffing over the surface of the meat. Roll up the meat and tie it at 2 inch intervals, turning in the end to make a neat roll. Reserve the marinade.

In a large flameproof casserole melt the butter or bacon fat, add the veal and brown slowly on all sides. Remove the veal, add the vegetables and cook, covered, for 5–7 minutes or until soft but not browned. Replace the veal, and add the reserved marinade. Cook until the liquid is reduced by half, then put in

the bouquet garni and pour in about two-thirds of the stock. Bring to a boil, cover and braise in heated oven for 2–2½ hours, basting occasionally.

After 1 hour, remove the lid and continue braising, basting from time to time and adding the rest of the stock if the liquid reduces rapidly. When the veal is tender and well glazed, remove it from the casserole; keep warm.

To make the sauce: discard the bouquet garni and stir chopped tomato or tomato purée into the mixture left in the casserole. Work the mixture through a fine sieve or in a blender, pour into a saucepan and bring to a boil. Adjust seasoning, thicken by whisking in kneaded butter, a small piece at a time, and cook until the sauce thickens. Stir in the cream and bring the sauce just back to a boil.

Sprinkle the tomato halves with salt, pepper and sugar and broil or bake in a moderate oven (350°F) for 8–10 minutes or until cooked. Fry or broil the bacon slices and drain them.

Remove the trussing strings from the veal, slice the meat

and arrange on a platter. Spoon a little of the sauce over the slices and serve the rest separately. Garnish the platter with tomatoes and bacon and serve gratin Dauphinois as an accompaniment.

Spread the stuffing on the breast of veal before rolling and tying it with string

Gratin Dauphinois

1½ lb baking potatoes, peeled
1 clove of garlic
salt and pepper
2 tablespoons butter
pinch of nutmeg
5 tablespoons grated Gruyère
    cheese
1½ cups milk
2 eggs

*Shallow baking dish
(1½–2 quart capacity)*

Gratin Dauphinois should be very smooth and melting in texture. It is a favorite dish in many of France's top restaurants where it is made with cream and egg yolks instead of milk and whole eggs.

For a richer version of this recipe, substitute heavy cream for the milk, use 4–5 egg yolks instead of the whole eggs and omit the garlic.

Method

Set oven at moderate (350°F).

Crush the garlic with a pinch of salt and work it into the butter. Spread this on the bottom and sides of the baking dish. Slice the potatoes thinly, if possible using a mandoline, and arrange them, overlapping, in the dish in neat rows. Season well, sprinkle the layers with nutmeg and 3 tablespoons of the cheese.

Scald the milk and pour it slowly onto the eggs, whisking constantly. Pour the mixture into the dish at the side. Scatter remaining cheese on top and place the dish in a water bath. Bake on top shelf of heated oven for 45–60 minutes or until the potatoes are browned and very tender when tested with a fork.

Watchpoint: the potatoes must be cooked very slowly to achieve the right melting texture; the milk and egg mixture must never boil or it will curdle.

Serve the gratin hot in the baking dish.

A **mandoline**, excellent for slicing vegetables, is a rectangular piece of wood, or metal, fitted with a plain or fluted sharp blade that can be adjusted to regulate the thickness of slices.

Pears Pralinées

4–5 ripe Anjou or Bartlett pears
light sugar syrup (made with
    1 cup sugar, 2 cups water
    and ½ split vanilla bean
    or 1 teaspoon vanilla extract)
4 plain sponge cupcakes
1–2 tablespoons Grand
    Marnier or kirsch (optional)

For praline
½ cup whole unblanched
    almonds
½ cup sugar

For cream
1 egg white
1 cup heavy cream, whipped
    until it holds a soft shape
1 tablespoon sugar (or to taste)

Method

To prepare sugar syrup: in a pan heat the sugar with the water until it is dissolved, add vanilla and simmer for 5 minutes.

Pare the pears and scoop out the cores through the bases with a teaspoon. Leave the stems intact. Put the pears into the syrup — it should cover them. Cover pan and poach 15–20 minutes.

When the pears are tender and thoroughly cooked, keep them in the syrup, turning occasionally, until they are cold.

To prepare the praline: put the almonds and sugar in a small heavy saucepan and cook over low heat. Let the sugar melt and begin to brown before stirring with a metal spoon, to toast the nuts on all sides. When the almonds are caramelized, cook 1–2 minutes longer to make sure the nuts are well toasted.

Pour the mixture into an oiled pie pan and leave until hard. Grind the praline with a cheese grater, pound it finely with a rolling pin or work it, a little at a time, in a blender. Keep the crushed praline in a screw-top jar until needed.

Slice the bottoms of the cupcakes, leaving a round to fit the base of each pear. Set these on a platter and moisten them with a little of the syrup in which the pears were poached. Sprinkle with Grand Marnier or kirsch, if you like. Drain the pears and place on the rounds of cake.

Whip the egg white until it holds a stiff peak, add it to the whipped cream with a little sugar and fold together. Stir in 2–3 tablespoons of the praline and spread a thick rough coating of the mixture on the pears, leaving the stems showing. Sprinkle more praline on top and chill well before serving.

An alternative, less rich way to serve the pears is with a sauce made from dried apricots (see Volume 4) in place of the cream. Coat the pears with sauce and scatter the top generously with praline before serving.

Sprinkle the pears with crushed praline after roughly coating them with the cream and praline mixture

Pears pralinées, with a whipped cream and egg white coating and topping of praline, are an attractive dessert

Alternative dessert

Mango Ice

2 large cans (15 oz each)
    mangoes
peeled rind and juice of 1 lemon
$\frac{1}{4}$ cup sugar
$\frac{1}{2}$ cup water

4 coupe or sherbet glasses

Method

Drain the syrup from the mangoes and reserve it. If you like, reserve a mango for decoration. Crush the mangoes thoroughly with a fork and put them in a quart measuring cup or bowl.

Put the lemon rind into a pan with the sugar and water. Heat until the sugar is dissolved, bring slowly to a boil and simmer 3–4 minutes. Stir in the strained juice of the lemon, remove the rind and pour the liquid into the measuring cup containing the mangoes. Add enough reserved mango syrup to make 1 quart.

Chill the mixture, pour it into ice trays, cover and place in the freezer. Freeze until mushy. Put it into a bowl, beat hard until it is smooth and freeze again.

Repeat the beating several times during the freezing process to avoid large ice crystals in the finished ice. When very stiff, cover the ice and freeze at least 1 hour before serving.

Serve the ice in chilled coupe or sherbet glasses and top with slices of reserved mango, if you like.

79

TROPICAL COOKING

Tropical food is pleasantly refreshing, not only because many fruits are used but also because few cooks feel like spending hours over a hot stove creating elaborate meals, so they tend to put handy ingredients together in unorthodox combinations with surprising success. Chicken, for example, is stewed with pork to make adobo — the rich national dish of the Philippines. Brazilians serve their favorite baked meat and beans with an orange salad, and Africans love to add peanuts to chicken and meats.

Many native dishes are highly spiced with chilies — in Asia and the Pacific other spices are added to temper them, but elsewhere chilies are added simply for their hot flavor. Experts argue about why hot dishes are so popular — some say pepper and spices help to preserve the food in a tropical climate, others claim pepper is added to induce sweating. Whatever the reason, native dishes in many countries seem impossibly fiery to Western palates.

Colonization has had a great influence on tropical food, particularly in Africa. Even though European settlers have long departed, it is still possible to identify their different nationalities by looking at local menus. Where Europeans have adapted native dishes to suit their own tastes — as with Indonesian rijstafel — flavors tend to be milder and textures lighter than in the native originals.

Savory stews of fish, meat and vegetables are a tropical staple, usually combined with some kind of starch such as rice in Southeast Asia, potatoes and corn in South America, and roots like cassava, sweet potatoes and peanuts in Africa and the Caribbean. Fruits are usually the main ingredients of desserts that are popular but the favorite way to serve fruit throughout the tropics is freshly cut — sometimes sprinkled with lime juice or sugar.

The following recipes from the Caribbean, South America, Pacific Islands and Australasia, Africa and Southeast Asia give a brief taste of the many varied dishes of the tropics.

Tropical Ingredients

Cassava (also called manioc and yucca) is an edible root that may be up to 3 feet long, and is obtainable from Latin American specialty stores.

Sweet cassava is eaten as a vegetable.

Bitter cassava, which comes from a related plant, is used to make tapioca; it is poisonous if eaten raw.

Manioc is meal made from bitter cassava. It is available in Latin American specialty stores.

Chayote, a tropical American vine has edible fruits and tubers. The pear-shaped, green or white fruits have one large seed and are obtainable from Latin American specialty stores.

Dasheen is a starchy root vegetable grown in tropical climates instead of potatoes. It is a variety of taro, a staple food in the Pacific and Southeast Asia. The roots, and sometimes the green leaves, are available in Southeast Asian stores.

Guava fruits come in various forms and sizes. The **white guava** has the best flavor; it is pear-shaped with a thin yellow skin and is the size of a hen's egg. The **red guava** is the shape of an apple. The **purple** or **strawberry guava** is larger — a round, dark red fruit with the flavor of strawberries. They are obtainable fresh in places like Puerto Rico where they are grown, and they are canned and preserved as jelly.

Papaya is a round fruit that can weigh up to 25 lb. It has a sweet, musky flavor and its juice can be used to tenderize meat. The seeds are attached to the hollow inside of the fruit. It is obtainable from specialty stores and good supermarkets.

Plantain, a variety of banana, always eaten cooked, is available in Latin American markets.

Ti leaves — trees or shrubs of the lily family with leaves in terminal tufts — are used in the South Pacific to hold food in place during cooking. They are available here at many florists.

Yams are vegetable tubers that can weigh as much as 100 lb. They are available in Latin American and Indian markets all year.

Yam is the name often incorrectly given to sweet potatoes; although they taste similar they come from a different plant family.

Coconut milk is made from the flesh of coconut. To make $\frac{1}{2}$ cup: steep $\frac{1}{2}$ cup freshly grated coconut in $\frac{1}{2}$ cup boiling water for 30 minutes, then squeeze through cheesecloth to extract all the 'milk'.

If fresh coconut is not available, pour $\frac{1}{2}$ cup boiling water over $\frac{1}{4}$ cup unsweetened shredded coconut and continue as above.

To Prepare Peppers, Chilies and Pimientos

Dried chilies: wash them in cold water, remove the veins, stems and seeds and cut the chilies into small pieces. Pour on about 6 cups boiling water per cup of chilies and add 2 teaspoons vinegar. Let soak for about 30 minutes and drain them, reserving the liquid if necessary.

Fresh chilies: soak them in cold salted water for 1 hour to remove some of the hot taste and drain. Use rubber gloves when handling fresh chilies as they contain oils that irritate the skin.

Canned chilies and pimientos: rinse them in cold water and drain, reserving the liquid, if necessary.

CARIBBEAN

The Caribbean is renowned for its rum — rum of all colors and strengths. Combined with local fruits it makes a huge variety of colorful drinks.

Less well known but equally exotic are the local stews that mix available ingredients in provocative combinations — like crab with okra and dasheen (a type of greens).

Ingredients for the following recipes are generally available here in Latin American stores.

Jamaican Pickled Fish

$1\frac{1}{2}$ lb steaks or fillets of kingfish, dolphin or any firm white fish
3 tablespoons olive oil
1 clove of garlic, peeled
1 small onion, finely chopped
1 cup white vinegar
1 fresh or canned chili, cored, seeded and chopped

Method
In a skillet heat the oil and fry the fish for 2–3 minutes on each side until brown.

Cut the garlic clove in half, rub it around a shallow dish (not metal) and place the fish in the dish. Bring the remaining ingredients to a boil, simmer 2 minutes and let cool.

Pour the liquid over the fish, cover and leave to marinate at least 5 hours, or up to 24 hours in the refrigerator, basting the fish occasionally. Serve chilled with potato salad.

Sweet Red Pepper Soup

3–4 bell peppers, cored, seeded and cut in pieces
$1\frac{1}{2}$ cups chicken stock
$1\frac{1}{2}$ cups heavy cream or evaporated milk
$1\frac{1}{2}$ tablespoons tomato paste
salt and pepper
$\frac{1}{4}$ teaspoon ground mace (or to taste)
$\frac{1}{3}$ cup coconut milk (see box)
little paprika (for sprinkling)

Method
Work the pieces of pepper through the fine blade of a grinder, add to the stock, cover and simmer 20 minutes. Stir in the cream or evaporated milk and tomato paste with salt, pepper and mace to

Ingredients for Cuban ajiaco include: piece of pork, ears of corn, (green) chayote and (dark brown) cassava roots, onions, garlic, green bell pepper, tomatoes, sweet potatoes, summer squash, plantains and limes

taste and bring just back to a boil. Chill.

Stir in the coconut milk and serve chilled with a sprinkling of paprika on each bowl.

Calalou
(Crab Stew with Okra and Greens)

$\frac{1}{2}$ lb crab meat
$\frac{1}{2}$ lb dasheen leaves, washed and chopped
$\frac{1}{2}$ lb okra, trimmed and sliced
thick slice (2 oz) of salt pork, diced
2 medium onions, sliced
thick slice (2 oz) of lean ham, diced
2 cloves of garlic, crushed
6 cups water
salt
black pepper, freshly ground
generous pinch of cayenne

This recipe, similar to Creole gumbo, is a cross between a soup and a stew. Calalou should be spicy and takes its name from calalou greens, known here as dasheen; fresh spinach is the closest substitute. Serve as a soup, or as a main dish with boiled rice.

Method
In a kettle gently fry the salt pork until browned. Add the onion and brown. Stir in the dasheen, ham and garlic and cook for about 1 minute or until the greens are limp. Add the water, okra, crab meat, seasoning and cayenne, cover and simmer 20–25 minutes or until it is thickened and the okra is tender. Taste the calalou for seasoning.

Ajiaco
(Cuban Pork and Vegetable Stew)

$1\frac{1}{2}$ lb pork, cut in $1\frac{1}{2}$ inch cubes
1 lb pork bones
3 quarts water
salt and pepper
2–3 cassava roots, peeled and cut in pieces
2 ears of corn, cut in pieces
3–4 sweet potatoes, peeled and cut in pieces
3–4 summer squash, trimmed
4 plantains, peeled and cut in pieces
1 medium chayote, cut in pieces
2 tablespoons oil
2 onions, chopped
1 green bell pepper, cored, seeded and chopped
2–3 tomatoes, peeled, seeded and chopped
2 cloves of garlic, crushed
juice of 2 limes

Method
Put the pork and bones with the water in a kettle, bring slowly to a boil and skim well. Add seasoning, cover and simmer $1\frac{1}{2}$ hours or until the meat is almost tender. Skim, then add the cassava, corn, sweet potatoes and squash and simmer 15 minutes longer. Add the plantains and chayote and simmer 10–15 minutes more or until all the vegetables are tender.

In a skillet heat the oil and fry the onion until golden brown. Add the green pepper and tomato with the garlic and seasoning and cook over low heat until very soft.

Take the summer squash from the stew and crush it to a pulp. Stir it into the tomato mixture and stir this back into the stew to thicken it. Discard the pork bones, add the lime juice, taste the stew for seasoning and serve with boiled rice.

Bien Me Sabe
(Puerto Rican Cake with Coconut Custard)

3 egg quantity of sponge cake,
  baked in an 8 inch springform
  pan (see Volume 6)
1½ cups grated fresh or
  unsweetened shredded
  coconut
¼ cup sweet white wine
3 cups milk
3 inch piece of cinnamon stick
2 whole cloves
8 egg yolks
½ cup sugar

Method
Sprinkle the wine over the cake on a platter and let stand.

Scald the milk with the coconut, add the cinnamon and cloves, cover and infuse over low heat for 15 minutes. Strain it through cheesecloth, squeezing to extract all the liquid.

Beat the egg yolks with the sugar until thick and light, stir in the hot coconut-flavored milk and return to the pan. Heat gently, stirring, until the custard coats the back of the spoon; do not boil.

Spoon the hot coconut custard over the sponge cake, cover and chill.

Barbados Guava Pie

5–6 ripe guavas or 1 can (16 oz)
  guavas, drained
½ cup sugar (optional)
1 cup water (optional)
¼ teaspoon ground nutmeg
juice of ½ lime
pie pastry, made with 1½ cups
  flour, ½ teaspoon salt, ¼ cup
  butter, ¼ cup shortening and
  3–4 tablespoons water
2 egg whites
¾ cup heavy cream, stiffly
  whipped (for serving) –
  optional

9 inch pie pan

Method
Make the pie pastry dough and chill.

If using fresh guavas, remove the blossom end and slice them. Heat the sugar with the water until the sugar is dissolved, bring to a boil and boil 2 minutes. Add the guavas to syrup and poach 10–15 minutes or until soft. Let cool, then drain.

Work fresh or canned guavas through a sieve or purée them in a blender. Stir the nutmeg and lime juice into the purée.

Set oven at hot (400°F). Roll out two-thirds of the pastry dough and line the pie pan.

Stiffly whip the egg whites, fold them into the guava purée and spread it in the pie shell. Roll out the remaining dough, cut it in strips and lay them across the pie in a lattice pattern, pressing the ends well into the pastry shell to seal them.

Bake the pie in heated oven for 10 minutes, turn down the heat to moderate (350°F) and bake 20–25 minutes longer or until the pie is browned and the filling begins to bubble through the lattice.

Serve the pie warm, with a bowl of whipped cream, if you like.

Grenadian Papaya Cream

Cut 1 ripe papaya in half, discard the seeds and scoop out the flesh. Work the flesh through a sieve or whip it to a foam in a blender. Stir in 1 teaspoon ground mace and ¼ cup sugar, adding more of both to taste; add 1 teaspoon vanilla and fold in 1 cup heavy cream, whipped until it holds a soft shape.

Pile the papaya cream in a glass bowl or 4 individual stemmed glasses and chill.

DRINKS

Banana Milk Punch

½ banana, peeled and cut in
  chunks
½ cup milk
2 oz light rum
2 teaspoons superfine (bar)
  sugar
juice of 1 lime
½ cup crushed ice
pinch of grated nutmeg
dash of angostura bitters

Serves 1 person.

Method
Combine all the ingredients in a blender and work until smooth and light. Pour into a 12 oz stemmed glass and serve.

Pineapple Orangeade

peel from 1 fresh pineapple
2 whole cloves
½ cup dark brown sugar
3 cups boiling water
1 cup fresh orange juice
2 slices of fresh pineapple
sprigs of mint (for garnish)

Serves 4 people.

Method
Rinse the pineapple peel and mix it with the cloves and sugar, pour over the boiling water, cover and let stand until cold. Strain and add the orange juice. Cut the core from the pineapple slices, finely shred the flesh and add to the orange mixture. Chill well, pour into four 8 oz glasses and top each with a sprig of mint.

Coconut Cocktail

½ cup coconut milk (see box, page 82)
juice of 1 lime
3 oz light rum
1 oz green crème de menthe
2–3 teaspoons superfine (bar) sugar
cracked ice
slice of lime (for garnish)

Serves 1 person.

Method
In a cocktail shaker combine all the ingredients with plenty of cracked ice, shake well, strain into a 10 oz glass, garnish with a slice of lime and serve.

Planter's Punch

3 oz dark rum
3 tablespoons fresh lime juice
pinch of nutmeg
dash of angostura bitters
1–2 teaspoons superfine (bar) sugar
crushed ice

For garnish
slice of orange
slice of lime
2 maraschino cherries
chunk of pineapple

Serves 1 person.

Method
In a glass stir the rum, lime juice, nutmeg, angostura bitters and sugar to taste until the sugar has dissolved.
Fill a tall glass with crushed ice, pour over the rum mixture and stir well. Spear the sliced orange, lime, cherry and pineapple (or any of these) on a toothpick, place in the glass and serve.

Colorful selection of refreshing Caribbean drinks includes from left to right: coconut cocktail, pineapple orangeade, planter's punch and banana milk punch

SOUTH AMERICA

The food of tropical South America is enormously varied because, though the coastal areas enjoy a tropical climate, the Central Andean plateau is chilly and bleak.

Cold weather products like corn, potatoes and llama meat are the Andean staples. Farther east the huge tropical rain forest of the Amazonian basin yields typically tropical products.

In the north, the mountains of Colombia and Venezuela are slashed by deep valleys and here tropical foods are still available in many areas. To the south, the Brazilian plains are excellent cattle country. West of the Andes, the coast of Peru with its cold Humbolt current is famous for an abundance of fish.

Feijoada (a rich stew) is the national dish of Brazil; the ingredients vary depending on the area, but beans, various kinds of sausage, pork, bacon, tongue, beef and pig's foot or ear are standard. The accompaniments are equally important and include orange salad, a shredded green vegetable resembling kale, toasted manioc meal, a hot pepper sauce and rice.

Feijoada
(Brazilian Baked Meat and Beans)

2–3 lb whole smoked tongue
1 lb chuck beef steak, cut in 1 inch cubes
4 cups dried black beans, soaked overnight and drained
1 onion, quartered
bouquet garni
6 peppercorns
1 lb fresh pork sausages
1 lb smoked garlic sausages such as mild Chorizo
1 pig's foot, split and washed
$\frac{1}{2}$ lb piece of Canadian bacon
2 tablespoons lard
3 medium onions, chopped
2 cloves of garlic, crushed
2 tomatoes, peeled, seeded and chopped
1 fresh or canned red chili, cored, seeded and chopped
salt and pepper

This recipe serves 8–10 people, as do all the accompaniments for feijoada.

Method
Put the tongue in a pan with the onion, bouquet garni, peppercorns and cold water to cover. Add the lid, bring to a boil and simmer $2\frac{1}{2}$–3 hours or until very tender when pierced with a skewer. Let cool to tepid in the liquid, then drain, skin the tongue and discard the bones and gristle from the root.

In a very large kettle cover the beans with about 2 quarts cold water, add the lid, bring to a boil and simmer 1 hour.

Prick the fresh sausages and put them in a large kettle with the smoked sausages and pig's foot. Cover with cold water, bring slowly to a boil, skim and simmer 20 minutes, then drain.

Add the pig's foot, peeled tongue and beef steak to the beans, cover and simmer $1\frac{1}{2}$ hours longer. Add the smoked and fresh sausages and Canadian bacon and simmer $\frac{1}{2}$ hour longer. At the end of cooking, the beans should be slightly soupy; add more water during cooking if the mixture looks dry.

Half an hour before serving, heat the lard in a skillet. Add the onion and garlic and cook until browned. Stir in the tomato and red chili and cook 1 minute longer.

Lift 1 cup beans from the pan, add to the skillet, crush to a paste, then stir in enough bean liquid to make a pourable mixture. Drain off and reserve $1\frac{1}{2}$ cups bean liquid to make the hot pepper sauce (see right). Stir the bean and onion mixture back into the beans to thicken and flavor the mixture, taste for seasoning and cook 15 minutes longer.

To serve, lift out the tongue and Canadian bacon, slice them and arrange down the center of a large hot platter. Cut the meat from the pig's foot and arrange it around the platter with the cubes of beef and both kinds of sausage.

Transfer the beans to a bowl, spoon a little bean liquid over the meats and serve with orange salad, shredded greens, toasted manioc meal, hot pepper sauce and Brazilian rice.

Accompaniments to Feijoada

Laranjas
(Orange Salad)

5–6 oranges
1 teaspoon sugar
salt and pepper

Method
With a serrated-edge knife, peel the skin and pith from the oranges and cut them in slices. Arrange them, overlapping, in a shallow serving dish, sprinkle with sugar and a little salt and pepper.

Arroz Brasileiro
(Brazilian Rice)

3 cups rice
2 cloves of garlic, bruised
$\frac{1}{4}$ cup oil
1 large onion, sliced
2 tomatoes, peeled, seeded and chopped
1 green bell pepper, peeled, seeded and chopped
6 cups boiling water
salt and pepper

Method
In a flameproof casserole fry the garlic in the oil until browned, then discard it. Add the onion and cook over low heat until soft but not browned. Add the rice and cook, stirring, until the grains are coated with oil and look transparent. Add the tomatoes and green pepper and cook 1 minute longer.

Pour in the boiling water, add seasoning, cover and bring back to a boil. Simmer 18–20 minutes or until all water is absorbed and the rice is tender.

Let the rice stand for 10

minutes, covered, before stirring with a fork.

Farofa
(Toasted Manioc Meal)

In a flameproof casserole or large skillet melt 3 tablespoons butter, add 2 cups manioc meal and break in 1 egg. Cook over medium heat, tossing and stirring constantly, for 8–10 minutes or until the manioc meal is golden brown and the grains are dry, separate and look like breadcrumbs.

Môlho de Pimenta
(Hot Pepper Sauce)

3–4 fresh or canned hot red
    chilies, cored, seeded and
    chopped
1 onion, chopped
$\frac{1}{4}$ cup peanut oil
$\frac{1}{4}$ cup vinegar
$1\frac{1}{2}$ cups liquid from cooking

Method
Pound the chilies and onion in a mortar and pestle, then beat in the peanut oil. Alternatively, purée the chilies, onion and oil in a blender. Stir in the vinegar and the bean liquid reserved from cooking feijoada.

Note: for details of how to prepare fresh or canned peppers, chilies and pimientos, see page 82.

Couve à Mineira
(Shredded Greens)

3 lb kale or collard greens,
    shredded
$\frac{1}{4}$ cup bacon fat
salt and pepper

Method
Blanch the greens in a large kettle of boiling salted water for 1 minute and drain.

In a large skillet heat the fat, add the greens and seasoning and fry them, tossing constantly, for 3–4 minutes or until they are just tender but still crisp.

Alfajor de Huaura
(Peruvian Pineapple Layer Cake)

4 cups flour
3 tablespoons confectioners'
    sugar
1 cup lard
$\frac{1}{2}$ cup milk
confectioners' sugar (for
    sprinkling)

For caramelized milk filling
2 cans (15 oz each) sweetened
    condensed milk
1 teaspoon vanilla

For pineapple filling
1 small pineapple, peeled,
    cored and grated
1 medium sweet potato
1 cup sugar

Method
To make the pastry dough: sift the flour onto a board or marble slab with the confectioners' sugar. Add the lard and rub in with the fingertips until the mixture resembles crumbs. Make a well in the center, add the milk and mix lightly, adding more milk if necessary to make a dough that is soft but not sticky. Knead the dough lightly, cover and chill 30 minutes.

Set the oven at moderately hot (375°F).

Divide the dough in 6 equal pieces; roll to 8-inch rounds, trim the edges with a sharp knife, using an inverted cake pan or a pan lid as a guide, and transfer the rounds to baking sheets. Chill 10 minutes, then bake 1–2 rounds at a time in the heated oven for 10–12 minutes or until lightly browned. Transfer them to a wire rack to cool.

To make the caramelized milk filling: in a deep saucepan submerge the 2 unopened cans of sweetened condensed milk in water and simmer for 3 hours.

Watchpoint: make sure the cans are completely covered with water at all times.

Let cool before opening the cans. Beat in the vanilla.

To make the pineapple filling: bake the sweet potato in a moderate (350°F) oven for 45 minutes or until tender. Let cool, then peel and mash it or work it through a sieve. Mix the grated pineapple with the grated sweet potato and sugar in a saucepan and stir over low heat 10–15 minutes or until the mixture is fairly smooth and just falls from the spoon. Let cool.

To finish: sandwich alternate layers of pastry with the fillings, leaving the top and sides plain. Sprinkle confectioners' sugar on the top and sides of the cake.

Hawaiian mango steak – the meat and fruit are cooked with onion and tomatoes in beer

PACIFIC ISLANDS AND AUSTRALASIA

The cooking of the Pacific Islands shows many influences – Chinese, Japanese, Korean and Polynesian blend happily in a huge variety of dishes.

The foods of Australasia have a British touch and Americans have left their mark on Polynesia and the Philippines.

I'A
(Fijian Steamed Fish with Sweet Potatoes)

4 whole red snapper or mullet (1 lb each)
4–5 large sweet potatoes, peeled, quartered and sharp edges trimmed
salt and pepper
juice of $\frac{1}{2}$ lemon
2 tablespoons oil
2 tablespoons butter

4 ti leaves or squares of foil

In Fiji the fish are wrapped in ti leaves but foil can be substituted.

Method
Set oven at moderate (350°F).

Wash and dry the fish, leaving the heads and tails on, and sprinkle with seasoning and lemon juice. Wrap them in ti leaves, fastening with string, or in buttered foil, sealing the edges tightly.

Set them on a wire rack in a roasting pan. Pour boiling water into the pan, put it in the heated oven and steam the fish for 15–20 minutes or until the flesh flakes easily when tested with a fork.

In a shallow flameproof casserole heat the oil and butter, add the sweet potatoes and brown them on all sides. Cover the pot and cook over low heat or bake in the oven with the fish for 10–12 minutes or until the potatoes are tender. Sprinkle with seasoning.

To serve, transfer the fish to a serving dish. If using ti leaves, serve the fish wrapped in them; if using foil, remove it, leaving the juices. Serve sweet potatoes separately.

Philippine Curried Eggs

4 eggs, beaten to mix
$\frac{1}{4}$ cup milk
$\frac{1}{2}$ teaspoon curry powder
salt
2 tablespoons butter
1 egg, beaten to mix (for coating)
$\frac{1}{2}$ cup grated fresh or unsweetened shredded coconut (for coating)
deep fat (for frying)

Serve as an accompaniment for curries.

Method
Beat the eggs, milk, curry powder and salt until thoroughly mixed.

In a small pan melt the butter, add egg mixture and cook gently, stirring constantly, until it scrambles and thickens enough to hold together. Cool, then shape the mixture into walnut-sized balls and chill thoroughly.

Brush the egg mixture balls with beaten egg and roll in grated coconut. Heat deep fat to 375°F on a fat thermometer, put the balls in a wire basket and fry them in hot fat until golden brown. Drain them on paper towels and serve.

Adobo
(Philippine Chicken and Pork Stew)

$3\frac{1}{2}$–4 lb roasting chicken
1 lb pork, cut 2 X 1 inch strips
1 teaspoon black pepper, freshly ground
2 cloves of garlic, crushed
$\frac{1}{2}$ cup cider vinegar
salt
2 cups water

Serves 6 people.

Method
Cut the chicken in half, discarding the backbone, then chop it into 12–14 pieces, including the bones, preferably using a Chinese cleaver. Thoroughly mix the chicken, pork, pepper, garlic and vinegar with a little salt, cover and let marinate 1 hour.

Transfer the mixture to a casserole, pour over the water, cover and cook very gently on top of stove or bake in a low oven (300°F) for 1–1$\frac{1}{2}$ hours or until the chicken and pork are very tender. Shake pan from time to time to prevent the meats from sticking.

When cooked, the liquid should be well reduced so the meats are almost dry. Serve with boiled rice.

Hawaiian Mango Steak

1$\frac{1}{2}$ lb piece round beef steak
2 mangoes
2 tablespoons oil
2 large onions, thinly sliced
3 tomatoes, peeled and sliced
1 bottle (11 oz) beer
salt and pepper

Method
In a skillet heat the oil and brown the beef steak on both sides. Arrange the sliced onion and tomato overlapping in a casserole and set steak on top.

Peel the mangoes and cut as much flesh as possible from the pits in slices. Crush the remaining flesh to a pulp with the juice.

Set the mango slices on top of the steak and pour over the pulp and beer. Sprinkle with salt and pepper, cover tightly and bake in a moderate oven (350°F) for 1$\frac{1}{2}$–2 hours or until the beef is very tender.

Note: for details of how to prepare fresh or canned peppers, chilies and pimientos, see page 82.

Hawaiian Pineapple Cake

1 fresh pineapple, peeled and
    sliced
1–2 tablespoons granulated
    sugar
$\frac{1}{3}$ cup butter
1 cup confectioners' sugar
2 egg yolks
$\frac{1}{2}$ cup chopped pecans or
    walnuts
1 teaspoon vanilla
1 package (10$\frac{1}{2}$ oz)
    brown-edged lemon wafers
$\frac{1}{2}$ cup heavy cream, stiffly
    whipped

*Pastry bag and medium star
tube*

Method
Shred half the pineapple slices,
discarding the core, to give 2
cups pulp and sprinkle the
remaining slices with 1–2
tablespoons sugar; cover and
chill.

Cream the butter, gradually
beat in the confectioners'
sugar until light and fluffy, and
then beat in the egg yolks, one
by one. Stir in shredded pineapple, nuts and vanilla.

Line an ice cube tray with
wax paper, spread a layer of
pineapple mixture in the bottom and cover with lemon
wafers. Continue adding layers
of pineapple mixture and
wafers until all are used, ending with wafers. Cover with
wax paper and chill overnight.

To serve, turn out the cake
onto a platter; arrange the
remaining half slices of pineapple around the edge.

Put the whipped cream into
a pastry bag fitted with a star
tube and decorate the cake
with rosettes.

Maori Cocoa Balls

$\frac{1}{2}$ cup butter
$\frac{1}{2}$ cup sugar
1 egg white
1$\frac{1}{2}$ cups self-rising flour
pinch of salt
6 tablespoons cocoa

For filling
1$\frac{1}{4}$ cups confectioners' sugar
about 1 tablespoon water

Makes 12 sandwiched balls.

Method
Set the oven at moderately
hot (375°F); grease a baking
sheet.

In a bowl cream the butter
and work in the sugar gradually until the mixture is light
and fluffy; beat in the egg
white.

On a sheet of wax paper sift
the flour, salt and cocoa. Stir
the flour mixture thoroughly
into the butter mixture and
shape the dough into rough
balls the size of walnuts.

Place the balls on the prepared baking sheet and bake
in heated oven for 8–10
minutes or until they brown
around the edges. Let the
balls stand on the baking
sheet to cool slightly, then
transfer to a wire rack to cool
completely.

To make the icing for the
filling: sift the confectioners'
sugar into a bowl and mix to a
smooth, stiff paste with 1 teaspoon of water at a time. Coat
the flat side of half the cookies
with icing and top with remaining cookies to make sand-
wiched balls.

*Tropical cookies shown are:
Maori cocoa balls, and
Ghanaian peanut balls topped with slivered almonds
(see recipe on page 92)*

AFRICA

The cooking of tropical Africa is very simple, generally consisting of soups and stews made with available ingredients.

Many of the ex-colonial nations have adopted the cooking style of their French, British and Portuguese colonizers, and the food of the east coast shows a strong Indian and Arab influence, particularly in the use of spices.

Boulettes de Poisson
(Senegalese Fish Balls)

For fish balls
1½ lb steaks or fillets of
   white fish
6 slices of white bread
½ cup chopped parsley
1 fresh or canned red chili,
   cored, seeded and chopped
3 tomatoes, peeled, seeded
   and chopped
1 clove of garlic, crushed
1 onion, chopped
salt

For cooking
3 tablespoons oil
2 onions, sliced
1 cup tomato purée
1 quart water
1 bay leaf
salt and pepper
3 carrots, quartered
2 white turnips, quartered
2 potatoes, quartered
2 sweet potatoes, quartered
1 small head of cabbage,
   cut in wedges
1 tablespoon white wine
   vinegar

Method
To make the fish balls: cut the fish in small pieces, discarding the skin and bones. Soak the bread in water for 5 minutes, then squeeze it dry. In a mortar and pestle pound to a smooth paste the parsley, chili, tomato, garlic and chopped onion, adding a large pinch of salt. Add the fish a little at a time and continue pounding until smooth.

Add the soaked bread, piece by piece, and continue pounding until the mixture is a fine paste. Alternatively, work all the ingredients in 4–5 batches in a blender until smooth.

Divide the mixture in pieces and roll into 1½ inch balls, oiling your hands so the mixture does not stick.

In a large skillet or shallow flameproof casserole heat the oil and fry the balls gently until golden brown all over, shaking the pan to prevent them from sticking. Take them out, add the sliced onion and cook until soft but not browned. Stir in the tomato purée with 1 quart water, bay leaf and seasoning. Add the carrots, cover and simmer 10 minutes.

Add the turnips, potatoes and sweet potatoes and simmer 10 minutes longer. Add the cabbage and the fish balls, simmer 10 minutes longer or until all the vegetables are tender. Discard bay leaf, add the vinegar and taste for seasoning.

Serve the fish balls and vegetables with boiled rice.

Ikokore
(Nigerian Fish Stew)

1 lb smoked fish such as
   Finnan haddie, smoked carp
   or smoked whitefish
½ lb uncooked, peeled shrimps
2 yams (about 1 lb)
1½ quarts water
2 tablespoons peanut oil
1 green bell pepper, cored,
   seeded and cut in strips
1 fresh or canned chili,
   cored, seeded and chopped
1 tomato, peeled, seeded and
   chopped
1 onion, chopped
salt and pepper

Method
Peel the yams and grate them; there should be 2–2½ cups pulp.

In a flameproof casserole bring the water to a boil, add the fish and simmer 10–15 minutes or until it flakes easily when tested with a fork. Lift the fish out with a slotted spoon and flake, discarding skin and bones.

Stir the grated yams into the boiling water and simmer 5 minutes. Add the peanut oil, flaked fish, bell pepper, chili, tomato, onion, and salt and pepper to taste and simmer 45–50 minutes or until the stew thickens. About 15 minutes before the end of cooking, add the shrimps.

Ethiopian Beef Stew

2 lb chuck or round beef steak,
   cut in 1 inch cubes
2 tablespoons oil
1 large onion, finely chopped
¼ teaspoon fenugreek seed,
   crushed
½ teaspoon ground allspice
¼ teaspoon ground nutmeg
1 clove of garlic, crushed
1 teaspoon finely chopped
   fresh ginger root
1 teaspoon ground red chili
   pepper
2 teaspoons paprika
1 cup water
salt and pepper

Method
In a large skillet or heavy flameproof casserole heat the oil and fry the onion until soft but not browned. Stir in the spices and cook very gently, stirring, for 2 minutes. Add the garlic, ginger root, chili pepper and paprika and stir 1 minute longer.

Add the beef, pour in the water, bring to a boil and season. Cover and cook very gently for 1½–2 hours or until the beef is very tender, adding more water if the mixture looks dry. Taste for seasoning and serve with Arab flat bread (pita – see Volume 12) or boiled rice.

Note: for details of how to prepare fresh or canned peppers, chilies and pimientos, see page 82.

Ghanaian Groundnut 'Chop'
(Chicken with Peanut Sauce)

$3\frac{1}{2}$–4 lb roasting chicken,
    cut in pieces
2 cups shelled fresh peanuts
    (groundnuts)
2 cups boiling water
1 cup coconut milk (see box,
    page 82)
2 tablespoons oil
1 onion, finely chopped
3 tomatoes, peeled, seeded
    and sliced
1 clove of garlic, crushed
salt and pepper
$\frac{1}{2}$ teaspoon paprika (optional)
$\frac{1}{4}$ teaspoon ground nutmeg
    (optional)
4 hard-cooked eggs, peeled

For serving
boiled rice
mango chutney
grated fresh coconut
red chilies, very finely chopped
sweet red onions, sliced and
    sprinkled with sugar and
    vinegar
sliced fresh banana or cooked
    plantain
foo foo (see right)

Method
Grind the peanuts and pound them to a smooth paste in a mortar and pestle, then gradually work in the boiling water. Alternatively, purée the peanuts with the boiling water in a blender. Simmer the mixture for 5–6 minutes or until the sauce is thick but still liquid, stir in the coconut milk and reserve.

In a skillet or shallow flame-proof casserole heat the oil and fry the chicken pieces until they are golden brown on all sides. Take them out, add the onion and fry until golden brown. Add the tomato and garlic and cook, stirring for 2–3 minutes until pulpy; stir in the peanut sauce with the seasoning, paprika and nutmeg, if used.

Bring just to a boil, put back the chicken pieces, and simmer, uncovered, for 30–40 minutes or until the chicken pieces are very tender, stirring from time to time to prevent them from sticking.

Five minutes before the end of cooking, add the eggs and spoon over the sauce to coat them; continue cooking until very hot. Serve with boiled rice and a variety of accompaniments as suggested.

Foo Foo
(Cassava Balls)

3 medium cassavas
    (about $1\frac{1}{2}$ lb)
pinch of cayenne
1 teaspoon salt

Makes 20–22 balls.

Method
Peel the cassavas and cut them in chunks. Put them in a pan with water to cover, add cayenne and salt, cover, bring to a boil and simmer 30–35 minutes or until the cassava is very soft. Drain the cassava, mash it, then beat until the mixture comes away from the sides of the bowl in a ball.

Moisten the palms of your hands and roll the mashed cassava into walnut-sized balls. Arrange the balls on a platter and cover tightly until ready to serve.

East African Chicken with Papaya

2 chickens (2–$2\frac{1}{2}$ lb each)
2 tablespoons butter
4 slices of bacon
1 firm ripe papaya
2 teaspoons prepared mustard
juice of 1 lemon
salt and pepper

Trussing needle and string

Method
Set oven at moderate (350°F).

Truss the chickens, spread them with the butter and lay the slices of bacon on top.

Halve the papaya, discard the seeds and cut a thin slice from the bottom so the halves sit firmly.

Place the papaya in a deep buttered casserole and spread the cut surfaces with mustard. Set the chickens on top, sprinkle with lemon juice and salt and pepper, cover and bake in heated oven for 50–60 minutes or until the chickens are very tender and the papaya is very soft.

To serve, split each chicken in half, discarding the backbones, and cut each piece of papaya in half. Serve each person half a chicken and a quarter of baked papaya.

Ghanaian Peanut Balls

1 cup blanched shelled peanuts
$2\frac{1}{2}$ cups flour
pinch of salt
1 cup butter
$\frac{3}{4}$ cup confectioners' sugar
2 teaspoons vanilla
2 tablespoons slivered almonds

Makes about 48 balls.

Method
Set the oven at hot (400°F).

Work the peanuts through the fine blade of a grinder and sift the flour with the salt.

Cream the butter and beat in the sugar until it is soft and light; add vanilla. Stir in the sifted flour with the ground peanuts.

Shape the dough into walnut-sized balls, set them on an ungreased baking sheet and stand a slivered almond in each one. Bake in heated oven for 10–12 minutes or until the balls are just beginning to brown. Transfer to a wire rack to cool completely.

These balls can be made ahead and stored in an airtight container for up to 1 week.

SOUTHEAST ASIA

The countries usually thought of as belonging to Southeast Asia include Indonesia, Malaysia, Thailand, Burma, Cambodia, Laos and Vietnam. As Southeast Asia is the home of spices, the cooking clearly reflects this. All these countries have distinctive styles of cooking, based on rice with a generous seasoning of spices.

The following recipes give examples of Southeast Asian food found in Indonesia, Malaysia and Thailand, while Hong Kong is a special case, its food having both a British and Chinese touch.

The following recipes and those on page 95 can all be served for an Indonesian rijstafel.

Indonesian rijstafel was developed by Dutch settlers in Indonesia who served banquets of rice dishes with a seemingly limitless succession of accompaniments each carried by a different servant. Today rijstafel is rarely served in traditional style but the same dishes are often displayed, buffet-style, for guests to serve themselves.

Nasi Ajam (Indonesian Chicken with Rice)

3½–4 lb roasting chicken or fowl
1 teaspoon ground coriander
1 bay leaf
thinly peeled rind of ½ lemon
½ teaspoon ground ginger
4 cups coconut milk (see box, page 82)
1½ cups rice

For garnish
spiced shredded 'omelet' (see right)
¼ cup finely chopped celery leaves
peeled rind of 1 lemon

Trussing needle and string

Method
Truss the chicken or fowl and put it in a kettle with the coriander, bay leaf, lemon rind, ginger and coconut milk. Cover, bring to a boil and simmer 35–40 minutes for the roasting chicken (or about 1¼ hours for the fowl) or until the bird is almost tender. Remove it, strain the broth and measure 3 cups.

Put the measured broth back in the kettle, add the rice, cover and bring to a boil. Replace the chicken in the pan, cover and simmer 20 minutes or until the rice has absorbed all the broth and both the rice and chicken are tender. Let stand 10 minutes, then spread the rice in a bowl and set the chicken on top.

Arrange the spiced shredded 'omelet' and chopped celery leaves on the rice, decorate the chicken with the lemon rind and serve with beef balls, shrimp and corn fritters, shrimp puffs, pork kebabs, raw vegetable salad and spiced fruit salad. (Recipes also given on page 95.)

Telor Gembung (Indonesian Spiced Shredded 'Omelet')

1 egg, beaten to mix
¼ teaspoon ground red chili pepper
pinch of salt
1 teaspoon oil

Method
Beat egg with chili pepper and salt. In a small skillet heat oil, add the egg and cook gently until set and browned underneath. Slide 'omelet' onto a plate, then roll and cut in shreds.

Krupuk (Indonesian Shrimp Puffs)

Shrimp chips are sold in Southeast Asian and Chinese stores. Fry them a few at a time in hot fat (375°F on a fat thermometer) — they will puff up at once. Drain them on paper towels.

Perkedel Djagung (Indonesian Shrimp and Corn Fritters)

4 ears of corn
1 small onion, grated
1 tablespoon finely chopped fresh coriander (Chinese — or Italian — parsley or cilantro)
½ teaspoon ground coriander
1 clove of garlic, crushed
1 tablespoon finely chopped celery tops
¼ cup finely chopped, cooked peeled shrimps
salt
2 eggs, beaten to mix
½ cup oil (for frying)

Method
Cut the corn kernels from the ears with a sharp knife and mix with the onion, fresh and ground coriander, garlic, chopped celery tops, shrimps and salt to taste. Stir in the beaten eggs.

In a skillet heat the oil and gently drop tablespoons of the fritter mixture into the oil. Fry over medium heat until golden, turn and brown on the other side. Drain on paper towels and keep hot while frying the remaining fritters.

Indonesian rijstafel dishes include from left: barbecued pork kebabs with wedges of lime, and shrimp and corn fritters. In the center are shrimp puffs, raw vegetable salad and spiced fruit salad. On the right the chicken with rice is garnished with spiced shredded omelet and chopped celery leaves, and below are fried beef balls

Perkedel Daging
(Indonesian Fried Beef Balls)

$\frac{1}{2}$ lb ground beef
1 cup freshly grated or unsweetened shredded coconut
1 onion, finely chopped
1 clove of garlic, crushed
$\frac{1}{2}$ teaspoon ground coriander
$\frac{1}{4}$ teaspoon ground cumin
$\frac{1}{2}$ teaspoon lemon juice
salt
1 egg
3–4 tablespoons oil

Method
If using dry coconut, pour 2 cups boiling water over it, let stand 15 minutes, then drain, discarding the liquid.

Mix the coconut with the beef, onion, garlic, spices, lemon juice and a little salt and beat in the egg to bind the mixture. Shape the mixture into balls the size of a walnut.

Heat the oil in a small skillet and fry the balls over medium heat a few at a time for 6–8 minutes, shaking the pan so they brown evenly. Drain them on paper towels and serve hot.

Note: for details of how to prepare fresh or canned peppers, chilies and pimientos, see page 82.

Asinan
(Indonesian Raw Vegetable Salad)

1 cucumber, peeled, seeded and sliced
1 cup fresh bean sprouts, washed and husks removed or 1 cup canned bean sprouts, drained and rinsed
1 cup shredded cabbage (optional)

For dressing
$\frac{1}{2}$ cup vinegar
$\frac{1}{2}$ teaspoon ground red chili pepper
pinch of sugar (optional)

Method
To make the dressing: mix the vinegar and ground pepper together.

Toss the vegetables in the dressing. Add a pinch of sugar if the mixture is very sharp, cover and let stand 1–2 hours before serving.

Saté Babi Manis
(Indonesian Barbecued Pork Kebabs)

1 lb lean pork, cut in $\frac{3}{4}$ inch cubes
1 teaspoon ground caraway seeds
1 teaspoon ground coriander
1 clove of garlic, crushed
$\frac{1}{2}$ teaspoon ground red chili pepper
2 tablespoons soy sauce
1 onion, chopped
1 tablespoon lemon juice
1 lime, cut in wedges (to serve)

6–8 bamboo skewers

Method
Mix all the ingredients, except the pork, in a bowl (not metal),

add the pork and mix well. Cover and let marinate 1–2 hours.

Spear the pieces of pork on the skewers and broil over charcoal for about 10–15 minutes or until the pork is tender, turning several times and basting with marinade. Serve the kebabs with lime wedges and saté sauce.

Satés, spicy little kebabs, are made in almost limitless variety in Indonesia. They are a popular snack or can be served as an entrée or as part of a rijstafel table. Beef, pork or chicken can be used.

Saos Saté Katjang
(Indonesian Peanut Saté Sauce)

$\frac{1}{4}$ cup shelled fresh peanuts
1 cup beef or chicken stock
$\frac{1}{8}$–$\frac{1}{4}$ teaspoon ground red chili pepper
1 tablespoon lemon juice
1 clove of garlic, crushed
1 tablespoon chopped fresh ginger root
salt

Method
Grind the peanuts with a rotary nut grater or pound them in a mortar and pestle until smooth. Bring the stock to a boil, stir in the ground peanuts with the remaining ingredients and salt to taste. Simmer, stirring constantly, for 10 minutes or until the sauce is thick enough to coat the back of a spoon.

Serve with barbecued pork kebabs.

Malaysian Eggs in Soy Sauce

4 eggs
$\frac{1}{4}$ cup soy sauce
1 teaspoon sugar
1 teaspoon oil
$\frac{1}{4}$ cup water

Serve these eggs as an appetizer with tomato or cucumber salad, or as an accompaniment to curry or rijstafel.

Method
Boil the eggs for 6 minutes, let stand in cold water until cool, then peel them carefully.

Mix the soy sauce, sugar, oil and water in a small saucepan, add the eggs and simmer 6 minutes. Take from the heat and let stand until cold, turning the eggs from time to time so they color evenly.

Leave the eggs in the soy sauce mixture until ready to serve, then drain them, discard sauce and cut in quarters.

Rudjak
(Indonesian Spiced Fruit Salad)

1 apple, cored and cut in thin slices
2 slices of fresh pineapple, cored and cut in chunks
1 orange, peeled and sectioned, with skin discarded
1 cucumber, peeled, seeded and cut in chunks

For dressing
1 tablespoon oil
1 tablespoon fresh lime juice
1 teaspoon ground cinnamon
$\frac{1}{2}$ teaspoon ground ginger

Method
Combine all the ingredients for the dressing. Mix the fruits and cucumber, toss with the dressing and pile in a bowl.

Sothi
(Malaysian Coconut Soup)

4 cups coconut milk (see box, page 82)
1 tablespoon oil
2 sweet red onions, finely sliced
2 fresh or canned green chilies, cored, seeded and chopped
1 star anise, crushed
$\frac{1}{4}$ teaspoon ground turmeric
1 cup ($\frac{1}{2}$ lb) uncooked, peeled shrimps
juice of 1 lemon
salt (to taste) – optional

Method

In a kettle heat the oil; cook the onion until soft but not browned. Add the chilies and anise and cook 2 minutes longer, stirring constantly. Add the turmeric and cook 1 minute longer.

Pour in the coconut milk and bring slowly to a boil, stirring. Simmer 5 minutes, add the shrimps, simmer 5 minutes longer. Take the soup from the heat, add the lemon juice, with salt, if necessary, and serve.

Kaeng Phet Nua
(Thai Meat Curry)

1$\frac{1}{2}$ lb lean chuck or round of beef, cut in 1$\frac{1}{2}$ inch cubes
3 cooked, peeled shrimps
2 cloves of garlic, crushed
grated rind of 1 lemon
1 tablespoon ground coriander
2 teaspoons ground turmeric
1 teaspoon ground caraway seed
$\frac{1}{2}$ teaspoon ground ginger
$\frac{1}{2}$ teaspoon ground red chili pepper
1 tablespoon vinegar
2 tablespoons vegetable oil
3–3$\frac{1}{2}$ cups coconut milk (see box, page 82)
1 teaspoon soy sauce
pinch of salt

Method

In a mortar and pestle pound the shrimps, garlic and lemon rind to a paste. Work in the spices and stir in the vinegar until smooth. Add to the beef cubes and toss and stir well until they are coated. Cover and let stand 1–2 hours.

In a skillet heat the oil and fry the beef cubes, a few at a time, until they are browned on all sides. Put the beef cubes in a pan, pour over 3 cups coconut milk, soy sauce and salt, cover and simmer gently 1$\frac{1}{2}$–2 hours or until the beef is tender. Remove the lid for the last 20–30 minutes cooking.

The curry should be fairly dry at the end of cooking but if it starts to stick during cooking, add more coconut milk. Taste for seasoning, adding more soy sauce, if necessary, and serve with boiled rice.

Hong Kong Kedgeree

$\frac{3}{4}$ lb smoked Finnan haddie
1 cup milk
3 hard-cooked eggs
3 tablespoons oil
$\frac{1}{2}$ cup shelled fresh peanuts
$\frac{1}{3}$ cup golden raisins
$\frac{1}{3}$ cup butter
1$\frac{1}{4}$ cups rice, boiled and drained
black pepper, freshly ground
1 tablespoon chopped parsley

Kedgeree is the English version of the Indian rice dish 'khichri'.

Method

Put the Finnan haddie in a baking dish, pour over the milk, cover and bake in a moderate oven (350°F) for 15–20 minutes or until the fish flakes easily when tested with a fork. Drain and flake fish, discarding the skin and bones.

Chop hard-cooked eggs, reserving 1 yolk for garnish.

In a skillet heat the oil and fry the peanuts until pale golden, add the raisins and cook $\frac{1}{2}$–1 minute longer or until the raisins are plump.

In a large flameproof casserole melt the butter, add the rice with plenty of pepper and heat until very hot, stirring with a fork. Add the chopped hard-cooked eggs, flaked fish, nuts and raisins and continue stirring and heating until very hot.

Pile kedgeree into a serving dish, sprinkle with chopped parsley and work the reserved egg yolk through a sieve on top of the kedgeree.

Hong Kong Almond Gelatin with Lychees

$\frac{1}{2}$ cup whole blanched almonds, ground
1 can (11 oz) lychees
2$\frac{1}{2}$ cups boiling water
2 envelopes gelatin
$\frac{1}{4}$ cup cold water
3 tablespoons sugar
$\frac{3}{4}$ cup evaporated milk or heavy cream
$\frac{1}{4}$ teaspoon almond extract (or to taste)

8 inch square cake pan

Method

Pour the boiling water over the almonds, cover and let stand in a warm place for 30 minutes. Strain through cheesecloth, squeezing to extract all the liquid. Discard residue and reserve liquid.

Sprinkle the gelatin over the $\frac{1}{4}$ cup cold water and let stand 5 minutes until spongy. Add the sugar and evaporated milk or cream to the almond liquid and heat gently until the sugar dissolves. Take from the heat, stir in the softened gelatin until it dissolves and let cool.

Add almond extract to taste, pour the mixture into the dampened cake pan and chill until firmly set. Cut the gelatin into 1 inch diamonds and pile them in a bowl. Pour over the lychees with their syrup and serve.

Note for details of how to prepare fresh or canned peppers, chilies and pimientos, see page 82.

Diamonds of almond gelatin float in a syrup with lychees for this Hong Kong dessert

Scoops of homemade vanilla ice cream are a perfect dessert (recipes on pages 103–104)

HOW TO MAKE ICE CREAM, SHERBET AND ICES

Ice cream is just one of a versatile family of iced desserts that ranges from meltingly rich parfaits made with whipped cream to refreshingly tart sherbet and ices.

There are two ways to make ice cream — in an ice cream churn freezer or in ice cube trays in the freezer. Churned ice cream has the best texture as the constant movement of the paddle prevents the large ice crystals that tend to form during freezing all but very rich mixtures like parfaits. When freezing in ice trays, most mixtures must be taken out and beaten once or twice during freezing but even this does not always result in a satin-smooth texture.

This feature includes recipes for ice cream, sherbet and ices, frappés and granités. Rich parfaits, iced mousses and molded iced desserts will be given in a future Volume.

Ice Cream Churn Freezers

The traditional ice cream churn freezer consists of a bucket for holding the ice with a metal container inside fitted with a paddle and cogs, leading to a handle. Turning the handle not only churns the mixture, but the paddle is shaped so it scrapes the sides of the container as it turns and mixes any frozen ice cream with the remaining mixture. Many bucket churns are now fitted with an electric motor instead of a hand crank.

Electric churns that fit inside the freezer, with a flex leading to a plug outside, are also available. They are convenient because no ice is needed but some home freezers do not reach a low enough temperature for these machines to operate efficiently and churning can take an hour or more. Churn freezers come in sizes that are measured by the capacity of the container.

Ice for Churning

Bucket churn freezers must be packed with ice so the container is tightly surrounded. Rock salt is mixed with the ice to lower the freezing temperature so ice cream freezes quickly.

The ice for packing the churn must be broken but the finely crushed ice from an electric ice crusher tends to melt too fast. Small ice cubes are excellent but large ones get wedged between the container and bucket.

Large ice cubes and block ice must be crushed by hand. To do this, set block on several layers of newspaper in a sink and chip into large pieces with an ice pick. Tie pieces of ice or ice cubes in a sack or large old cloth and pound them with a hammer or mallet until broken into convenient-sized pieces.

To Prepare a Churn Freezer

Scald the paddle, container and lid so they are very clean with no trace of odor and dry them; chill before packing with ice. If the bucket has not been used for a long time and is made of wood, soak it for 1 hour in water to swell the wood and prevent leaking.

After use, thoroughly wash the container, paddle and lid. Wipe the cogs and handle, carefully removing any pieces of salt; rub metal parts with a little oil to prevent them from rusting. Store the container with the lid off.

To Pack a Churn Freezer

Set the container and its lid in the bucket and assemble machine by attaching bar and motor or handle over container to hold it in position.

Fill the sides of the bucket (around container) with ice and rock salt, using about 1 part salt to 3 parts ice, and pack the mixture down well

Some of the equipment for making ice cream (from top left) – ice cube trays; pail and ice pick; nylon sieve; stainless steel bowl; ice cream churn freezer; electric ice cream churn to use in freezer; ice cream bombe molds and a scoop

with the handle of a wooden spoon. Continue until the ice comes within 1 inch of the container lid.

Brush any ice or salt from the container lid and carefully lift off the bar and lid.

Fill the container about two-thirds to three-quarters full with ice cream mixture and add the paddle. Replace the lid and seal the edge with a little butter or shortening. Replace the bar and motor or handle and, as far as possible, seal the gap where the top of the paddle enters the container with more butter or shortening.

Alternatively, seal the container by placing a sheet of foil or wax paper on top, pierce a hole for the top of paddle and add the lid. Fill the bucket with ice and salt to the level of the container lid, then start the motor or turn the handle.

To Freeze Ice Cream in a Churn Freezer

If cranking by hand, start turning slowly, then turn faster as the mixture begins to feel stiff, then slower as it becomes firm. Churning time can vary from 8—15 minutes, depending on the quantity and type of mixture.

Most electric motors will start to 'labor' when the ice cream is stiff and some machines have an automatic cut-off mechanism. Keep the bucket filled to the top with ice and salt during churning.

When the ice cream is stiff, stop churning and pour off water from the hole in the side of the bucket. Wipe the ice and salt from the container lid, then remove the bar. Carefully lift off the container lid, pull up the paddle with one hand, while holding

down the container with the other and scrape ice cream from the paddle back into the container with a spatula.

Ice cream must be left to mellow in the container or in the freezer at least 1 hour and preferably 3—4 hours after making. This improves the flavor and texture, particularly of rich cream mixtures.

If leaving the mixture in the container, push it down from the sides into the bottom, cover the top with a double sheet of foil or wax paper and add the lid. Block the hole with a piece of paper or small cork and fill the bucket with more ice and salt to cover the container completely. Cover the bucket with a sack or thick cloth and let stand. Ice cream can be left for several hours but the ice and salt will need replacing.

Alternatively, the container of ice cream can be stored in the freezer or the ice cream can be packed into chilled molds or heat-resistant serving bowls, covered and stored in the freezer.

To Freeze Ice Cream in Ice Cube Trays

Scald and chill the ice trays. Pour the ice cream mixture into the trays and freeze as quickly as possible in the freezer. Be sure the freezer is turned to maximum coldness.

As soon as the mixture is slushy, remove it and beat it with a chilled beater in a chilled bowl until smooth. Replace it in the freezer and repeat the beating 2—3 times, until the mixture is fairly firm. Then smooth the top, cover with foil or wax paper and leave at least 1 hour to mellow in the freezer.

Ice cream made in ice trays cannot be stored as long as ice cream made in a churn freezer because the texture deteriorates more rapidly.

To Store Ice Cream

If storing ice cream for more than a few hours, pack it into chilled metal molds or heat-resistant serving dishes, cover tightly with freezer wrap and store in the freezer. Use simple shapes, such as a melon mold, because complicated shapes do not unmold well.

Sherbet and ices may be packed into individual heat-resistant glasses and frozen ready for serving. Fruit shells, such as hollowed-out oranges, lemons, tangerines and melons, are particularly attractive containers for fruit sherbet and fruit ice cream.

Rich ice cream can be stored in the freezer for 2—3 months without harm, but mixtures like sherbet that contain a high proportion of water, tend to crystallize on standing and should be used within 2—4 weeks.

To Serve Ice Cream

To turn out molded mixtures, dip the mold quickly into cold water, wipe the mold and turn the ice cream out onto a platter. For formal occasions, the ice cream should be unmolded onto a folded white napkin on a silver platter; otherwise use any dish that is thoroughly chilled.

If the ice cream is not molded or packed into a serving bowl, it looks most attractive shaped into balls with an ice cream scoop. Dip the scoop into a pitcher of cold water, then into the ice cream. When the scoop is full, level it off with a knife or against the side of the container and unmold the ice cream ball into a chilled dish, preferably a silver or glass one. Continue until all the ice cream is shaped.

Sherbet and ices containing a relatively high proportion of water can become very hard if stored for more than a few days, so let them soften in the refrigerator for 1 hour before serving.

Note: when chilling glass serving dishes or cups, do not leave them in the freezer or refrigerator too long or they may crack. When freezing ice cream and iced desserts in glasses, use heat-resistant glasses.

Packing a churn freezer

1 *Set the container and its paddle inside the bucket; fix the handle over the container*

2 *Fill around the container with a mixture of ice and rock salt; pack it down with a spoon*

3 *Before churning, lift off the bar and lid and pour the ice cream mixture into the container*

4 *Seal the container by covering it with foil or wax paper and make a hole for paddle; add the lid*

Sugar Content of Ice Cream

The proportion of sugar in a mixture to be frozen is important so follow recipe carefully.

Too sweet a mixture will not freeze; one that is not sweet enough will be tasteless and hard.

This can be corrected to a certain extent by adding more sugar after the mixture is frozen but it is better to have the proportions of the basic mixture right, particularly for sherbet.

Note: never add more than 1–2 tablespoons liquor to a mixture as alcohol also prevents freezing.

Points to remember

1 Fruit juices for sherbet and ices should be strained to remove any pulp; straining is not necessary for any other types of ice cream.

2 Taste the basic mixture before freezing, particularly when using fruit, as acid fruits usually need extra sugar. The mixture should be sweet because the flavor is diminished by freezing. If the taste seems excessively sweet, add a pinch of salt.

3 To freeze the ice cream as quickly as possible, chill the container, lid, paddle and ice cream mixture before packing the churn with ice.

4 Do not attempt to freeze too much mixture at once. As it freezes, the mixture will expand by as much as a quarter of its volume and the texture will not be as light if it is too tightly packed. Sherbet and other mixtures with a high proportion of water will expand less than cream mixtures.

5 Take great care when lifting the lid of the container before and after freezing so no salt falls into the ice cream. A grain of rock salt will ruin the flavor.

6 To make hand cranking easier, set the churn on a low stool or table covered with newspaper.

7 Do not strain a motor or crank handle if it will not turn easily because this can damage the cogs. Stop turning and see if ice or salt is causing the blockage.

8 Crush plenty of ice before you start freezing. Freezing is slowed down considerably if the bucket is not kept full of ice and the bucket will need constant replenishment, particularly on hot days.

9 Freshly frozen mixtures thaw very quickly, so handle them as fast as possible and always thoroughly chill any mold or equipment that comes in contact with the mixture.

ICE CREAM

A churn freezer makes superbly smooth ice cream but excellent results can be obtained by freezing a really rich mixture containing whipped cream in ice trays.

The best ice cream, often called custard or French ice cream, is based on eggs and milk — either a custard or mousse made of egg yolks beaten with hot sugar syrup until thick. In some recipes flour may be added as well as eggs to thicken the mixture but the finished ice cream is less smooth and rich.

When the basic mixture is cold, cream is added; the heavier the cream the richer the ice cream will be. Light cream can be used with an egg mousse base that is frozen in a churn freezer; but heavy cream, whipped until it holds a soft shape, should be added to any ice cream frozen in ice trays to give a smooth texture. Heavy cream is also best for ice cream with an egg custard base that is frozen in a churn freezer.

Ice cream can be flavored with almost anything you can think of — vanilla, chocolate, coffee and strawberry are obvious favorites but some unexpected combinations like wholewheat bread with vanilla ice cream are astonishingly good.

Vanilla Ice Cream 1 (Custard Base)

2 eggs
2 egg yolks
$\frac{1}{3}$ cup sugar or vanilla sugar (made by leaving a vanilla bean in an airtight jar of sugar for several days)
$2\frac{1}{2}$ cups milk
1 vanilla bean, split or
   $1\frac{1}{2}$ teaspoons vanilla extract
1 cup heavy cream, whipped until it holds a soft shape

To add extra flavor to the ice cream, use vanilla sugar instead of vanilla bean or extract. This recipe is best made in a churn freezer. Makes about 1 quart.

Method

Beat the eggs with the egg yolks until mixed and whisk in the sugar until the mixture is smooth but does not start to thicken. Scald the milk and, if using vanilla bean, cover and infuse 8–10 minutes. Let cool, covered, and strain the milk into the egg mixture, stirring vigorously. Cool, then strain the custard and add vanilla extract, if using.

Stir the whipped cream into the custard and taste for flavor, adding more vanilla extract if necessary. Chill thoroughly and freeze in a churn freezer or ice trays.

Vanilla Ice Cream 2
(Egg Mousse Base)

3 cups light cream or 1½ cups
  light cream and 1½ cups
  heavy cream
1 vanilla bean, split or
  1½ teaspoons vanilla extract
⅓ cup sugar
⅓ cup water
4 egg yolks

This recipe is excellent for freezing in ice trays, particularly when using whipped heavy cream. Makes about 1 quart.

Method
Scald the light cream and vanilla bean, if using; cover and infuse 8–10 minutes. Let cool, covered, and strain.

In a small pan dissolve the sugar in the water over low heat, then bring to a boil and boil steadily until the syrup forms a thread between finger and thumb when a little is lifted on a spoon (230°F–234°F on a sugar thermometer).

Meanwhile, beat the egg yolks until they are light and slightly thickened. Let the bubbles in the syrup subside and pour it gradually into the egg yolks, beating constantly. Continue beating until the mixture is cool and thick. Stir in the cooled cream and vanilla extract, if using.

Whip the heavy cream, if using, until it holds a soft shape, add to the mixture, taste for flavor and add more vanilla extract, if necessary. Chill thoroughly and freeze in a churn freezer or ice trays.

Note: a recipe for meringue glacé maison including a white coffee ice cream will be given in a future Volume.

Chocolate Ice Cream 1

Use the recipe for vanilla ice cream 1 (see page 103), but melt 7 squares (7 oz) semisweet chocolate, chopped, in the scalded milk before continuing as for the vanilla ice cream.

Chocolate Ice Cream 2

7 squares (7 oz) semisweet
  chocolate, coarsely chopped
3 cups light cream
¼ cup sugar
¼ cup water
3 egg yolks, beaten to mix
1 teaspoon vanilla or
  1 tablespoon rum or brandy

Makes about 1 quart.

Method
Heat the chocolate with the cream, stirring until the chocolate is melted. Bring it to scalding point, take from the heat, cover and let cool.

In a small pan dissolve the sugar in the water over low heat, then bring to a boil and boil steadily until the syrup forms a thread between finger and thumb when a little is lifted on a spoon (230°F–234°F on a sugar thermometer).

Meanwhile beat the egg yolks until they are light and slightly thickened. Let the bubbles in the sugar syrup subside and pour it gradually into the egg yolks, beating constantly. Continue beating until the mixture is cool and thick.

Stir in the cool chocolate cream and the vanilla, rum or brandy. Chill thoroughly and freeze in a churn freezer or ice trays.

Chocolate Ice Cream 3

This ice cream is very suitable for making in ice trays.

Use the previous recipe for chocolate ice cream 2, but melt 7 squares (7 oz) of chocolate, chopped, in only 1½ cups light cream before making the mixture.

When cold, whip 1½ cups heavy cream until it holds a soft shape, stir into the chocolate mixture and freeze in a churn freezer or in ice trays.

Chocolate Chip Ice Cream

Make vanilla ice cream 1 (see page 103) or chocolate ice cream 2. When the ice cream is thick, add 1 cup semisweet chocolate chips, coarsely chopped. Churn until firm.

Coffee Ice Cream

Use vanilla ice cream 1 (see page 103) or 2, but omit the vanilla bean. Use only 1 teaspoon vanilla extract and add to it 1–1½ tablespoons dry instant coffee. Continue as for vanilla ice cream.

Praline Ice Cream

½ cup whole unblanched
  almonds
½ cup sugar
about 1 quart vanilla ice
  cream 1 (see page 103) or 2

Method
In a small heavy-based pan gently heat the almonds and the sugar until the sugar melts, shaking the pan occasionally. When the sugar turns a pale golden brown, stir the mixture with a metal spoon and continue cooking until it is a dark brown.

Pour the mixture at once onto an oiled baking sheet and let cool until cold and hard. Grind the praline in a rotary cheese grater or a grinder or work in a blender, a little at a time.

Stir the crushed praline into the vanilla ice cream and freeze in a churn freezer or ice trays.

Pistachio Ice Cream

1 cup shelled pistachios
squeeze of lemon juice
about ¼ cup heavy cream

For vanilla ice cream
3 cups light cream or 1½ cups
  light cream and 1½ cups
  heavy cream
⅓ cup sugar
⅓ cup water
4 egg yolks
few drops of green food
  coloring

Makes about 1 quart.

Method
Grind pistachios in a rotary cheese grater or work in a blender until fine. Pound them in a mortar and pestle with the lemon juice and enough heavy cream to make a stiff but smooth paste.

Make the ice cream as for vanilla ice cream 2 and add the pistachio paste with the egg yolks. Gradually beat in the hot syrup and continue as directed in the recipe but omit vanilla flavoring. Color the pistachio mixture with a few drops of green food coloring.

A selection of homemade ice cream and sherbets (from left): scoops of vanilla ice cream; pineapple sherbet set in two pineapple halves; more scoops of vanilla ice cream; grapefruit with mint sherbet and a dish of chocolate chip ice cream

Caramel Pecan Ice Cream

1 cup pecans, coarsely chopped
$\frac{1}{2}$ cup sugar
about 1 quart vanilla ice
  cream 1 or 2 (see pages
  103–104)

Method

In a small heavy-based pan gently heat the pecans and sugar until the sugar melts, shaking the pan occasionally. When the sugar turns a pale golden brown, stir the mixture with a metal spoon to coat nuts and continue cooking until a rich caramel. Pour it at once onto an oiled baking sheet and let cool until hard.

Crush the mixture in a mortar and pestle or with the end of a rolling pin in a bowl so the caramel is crushed in very small pieces but large pieces of pecan still remain. Stir it into the vanilla ice cream when thick and freeze in a churn freezer or ice trays.

Fruit Ice Cream

$2\frac{1}{2}$ cups fruit purée
2 cups light cream
$\frac{1}{2}$ cup sugar
$\frac{1}{2}$ cup water
3 egg yolks

Makes about $1\frac{1}{2}$ quarts.

Method

To make the ice cream: scald the cream, cover and let cool. In a small pan dissolve the sugar in the water over low heat, then bring to a boil and boil steadily until the syrup forms a thread between finger and thumb when a little is lifted on a spoon (230°F– 234°F on a sugar thermometer).

Beat the egg yolks until they are light and slightly thickened. Let the bubbles in the sugar syrup subside and gradually pour into the egg yolks, beating constantly. Continue beating until the mixture is cool and thick. Stir in the cooled cream and fruit purée. Chill thoroughly and freeze in a churn freezer or in ice trays.

To make Fruit Purée

Strawberry: hull about 1 quart strawberries and work them through a sieve or purée in a blender. Add the juice of $\frac{1}{2}$ lemon and sweeten to taste with confectioners' sugar.

Raspberry: work about 1 quart raspberries through a sieve or purée in a blender and strain to remove seeds. Add 1 tablespoon kirsch, if you like, and sweeten to taste with confectioners' sugar.

Blueberry: work 3 cups cooked blueberries through a sieve or purée in a blender. Add the juice of $\frac{1}{2}$ lemon and sweeten to taste with confectioners' sugar.

Cranberry: work 3 cups cooked cranberries through a sieve or purée in a blender. Sweeten to taste with confectioners' sugar.

Peach: peel and pit 3 large peaches and work through a sieve or purée in a blender. Add $\frac{1}{4}$ teaspoon almond extract and sweeten to taste with confectioners' sugar.

Apricot: work 3 cups cooked apricots through a sieve or purée in a blender. Add $\frac{1}{4}$ teaspoon almond extract or juice of $\frac{1}{2}$ lemon and sweeten to taste with confectioners' sugar.

Banana: peel and crush 3 bananas; work them through a sieve or purée in a blender. Add juice of 1 orange and sweeten to taste with confectioners' sugar.

Wholewheat Bread Ice Cream

5–6 slices of dry wholewheat
  bread, crusts removed
2 tablespoons sugar
about 1 quart vanilla ice
  cream 2 (see page 104)

Sherbet glasses

Method

Make the slices of wholewheat bread into breadcrumbs and sprinkle with sugar, spread on a tray or baking sheet and bake in a moderately hot oven (375°F) for 8–10 minutes or until well browned. Let crumbs cool — there should be 6 tablespoons.

Make vanilla ice cream and, when thick, stir in the crumbs, and continue freezing until very firm.

To serve, shape the ice cream into balls with a scoop, pile into the chilled sherbet glasses and serve with Melba or caramel sauce.

Note: sauces for serving with ice cream are given in Volume 9.

Tutti Frutti

vanilla ice cream 2
  (see page 104)
1 tablespoon maraschino
  liqueur
1 teaspoon vanilla
$\frac{1}{2}$ cup red maraschino cherries,
  drained and chopped
$\frac{1}{4}$ cup green maraschino
  cherries, drained and
  chopped
2 slices of candied pineapple,
  chopped
4 dried uncooked apricots,
  chopped
$\frac{1}{2}$ cup browned, slivered
  almonds

To finish (optional)
candied fruits, sliced
$\frac{1}{2}$ cup heavy cream (softly
  whipped)

*Large loaf pan (9 X 5 X 3
  inches); pastry bag and
  medium star tube (optional)*

Method

Make vanilla ice cream 2 but substitute maraschino liqueur and 1 teaspoon vanilla for the $1\frac{1}{2}$ teaspoons vanilla specified. Freeze in a churn freezer or in ice trays until the mixture is thick. Add the maraschino cherries, candied pineapple, apricots and almonds. Freeze the mixture until firm, then fill into the loaf pan. Cover and store in the freezer.

To serve, unmold the ice cream onto a platter and decorate the top, if you like, with more sliced candied fruits and pipe rosettes of whipped cream around the edge.

Tutti frutti is garnished with candied fruits and rosettes of cream

SHERBET

Sherbet, the ancestor of all ice cream, was created by the Turks, who refreshed their guests with a frozen fruit drink called 'sharbah'.

Sherbet used to be served in the middle of long banquets to clean and refresh the palate in preparation for the rich courses to follow; now it is sometimes served as an appetizer or as a popular end to a rich dinner.

Fruit juice or purée, liqueurs or heavy wines such as sherry and Sauternes make the basic mixture. This is sweetened with sugar or sugar syrup and some kind of stabilizer such as egg white or gelatin is needed. If gelatin is used, it is included in the basic mixture, but when adding egg white, the mixture is frozen until slushy, then a very small quantity of whipped egg white is added and freezing is continued until the mixture is firm. Sometimes meringue italienne is added to sherbet to give a particularly soft texture.

Sherbet is best when churned while it is freezing, although it can be frozen in ice trays if gelatin as well as egg white is added to the mixture.

To Freeze Sherbet

Make the sherbet mixture according to the recipe and chill thoroughly.

To Freeze in a Churn Freezer

Pour the mixture into the container, surround with ice and salt, cover with foil or wax paper, add the lid, bar and motor or handle and let stand 5 minutes.

Stiffly whip the egg white.
Watchpoint: very little egg white is needed, although the quantity varies with the consistency required in individual recipes. Half an egg white is the smallest amount possible to beat, but all of even this small amount may not be needed.

Start the motor or, if churning by hand, turn slowly and steadily for about 5 minutes or until the mixture begins to feel stiff. Wipe the lid of the container, remove the bar and carefully lift off the lid. When the mixture is slushy (partly set), add the egg white, replace the lid and bar and continue churning until the sherbet is stiff. If the mixture has not begun to set, continue churning a few minutes longer before adding the egg white.

When very stiff, lift out the paddle and pack down the sherbet or transfer it to chilled molds or glasses as directed in general instructions on pages 100–101.

To Freeze in Ice Trays

For every quart of sherbet mixture, sprinkle 1 envelope gelatin over $\frac{1}{4}$ cup sugar syrup or water and let stand 5 minutes or until spongy. Dissolve the gelatin over a pan of hot water and stir into the sherbet mixture. Let cool.

Pour the mixture into ice trays and freeze, with the freezer turned to maximum coldness, until the mixture is slushy. Turn it into a chilled bowl, beat with a chilled beater until smooth, then beat in the egg white. Cover tightly with foil or wax paper and chill again, beating once or twice more to break up ice crystals as the sherbet freezes.

When very firm, pack the sherbet into chilled molds or glasses, or leave in ice trays and cover tightly. Turn the freezer back to normal setting.

Lemon Sherbet 1

grated rind of 3 lemons
$\frac{1}{2}$ cup lemon juice
1 cup sugar
3 cups water
1 envelope gelatin and
    $\frac{1}{4}$ cup water (optional)
$\frac{1}{2}$ egg white

Makes about 1 quart.

Method
Put the lemon rind, sugar and water in a pan, heat gently until sugar dissolves, then bring to a boil and simmer 5 minutes. Strain into a bowl, add lemon juice, mix well and taste for sweetness.

If freezing the sherbet in ice trays, sprinkle the gelatin over $\frac{1}{4}$ cup water, let stand 5 minutes until spongy, dissolve it over a pan of hot water and stir into the lemon mixture.

Chill the mixture and freeze in a churn freezer or ice trays. When slushy, stiffly beat the egg white; add 1 tablespoon of it to the sherbet. Continue freezing until it is firm.

Lemon Sherbet 2

4 large lemons
1 cup sugar
3 cups water
1 tablespoon kirsch
1 envelope gelatin and
    $\frac{1}{4}$ cup water (optional)
4 bay leaves (for serving)

For meringue Italienne
1 egg white
$\frac{1}{4}$ cup sugar
$\frac{1}{4}$ cup water

Makes about $1\frac{1}{2}$ quarts.

Method
Cut the tops off the lemons and scoop out the flesh with a teaspoon or grapefruit knife; reserve the shells and tops and chill them. Crush the flesh in a sieve to extract the juice and measure it — there should be $\frac{3}{4}$ cup.

Heat the 1 cup sugar with 3 cups water until dissolved, bring to a boil and simmer 5 minutes. Add to the lemon juice and kirsch, mix well and taste for sweetness.

If freezing the sherbet in ice trays, sprinkle the gelatin over $\frac{1}{4}$ cup water, let stand 5 minutes until spongy, dissolve it over a pan of hot water and stir into the lemon mixture. Chill the mixture.

To make the meringue italienne: dissolve the sugar in the water in a small pan, bring it to a boil and simmer until the syrup forms a thread between finger and thumb when a little is lifted on a spoon (230°F–234°F on a sugar thermometer).

Stiffly beat the egg white and pour in the hot sugar syrup, beating constantly; continue beating until the meringue is stiff and glossy; reserve it.

Freeze the lemon mixture in a churn freezer or ice trays. When slushy, beat in the meringue Italienne and continue freezing until it is firm.

When very firm, fill the sherbet into the chilled lemon shells, mounding the tops, and set a lemon lid on each shell. Freeze the sherbet until very firm, then seal in plastic wrap or foil, if storing. Insert a bay leaf in the lid of each shell before serving to resemble a lemon leaf.

Orange Sherbet

3 large oranges
peeled rind and juice of 1 lemon
$\frac{3}{4}$ cup sugar cubes
3 cups water
1 envelope gelatin and
$\quad \frac{1}{4}$ cup water (optional)
$\frac{1}{2}$ egg white

Makes about $1\frac{1}{2}$ quarts.

Method
Rub about $\frac{1}{4}$ of the sugar cubes over the rinds of the oranges to absorb the zest (oil) until saturated. Squeeze juice from oranges and add to lemon juice — there should be $1\frac{1}{2}$ cups.

Put the lemon rind with the water and remaining sugar in a pan and heat gently until the sugar dissolves. Bring to a boil and simmer 5 minutes. Take from the heat, add the orange-soaked sugar cubes and heat gently until the sugar is dissolved. Stir the sugar syrup into the orange and lemon juice and taste for sweetness.

If freezing sherbet in ice trays, sprinkle gelatin over $\frac{1}{4}$ cup water, let stand 5 minutes or until spongy, dissolve it over a pan of hot water and stir into the orange mixture.

Chill the mixture and freeze in a churn freezer or ice trays. When the mixture is slushy, stiffly beat the egg white and add 1 tablespoon to sherbet. Continue freezing until firm.

Pineapple Sherbet

1 large pineapple
1 quart fresh strawberries, hulled, or raspberries, picked over
sugar (for sprinkling)
8–10 strawberry or vine leaves (for decoration)

For sherbet
$\frac{3}{4}$ cup sugar
peeled rind of 1 lemon
$2\frac{1}{2}$ cups water
$\frac{1}{4}$ cup lemon juice
$\frac{1}{2}$ envelope gelatin and
$\quad$ 2 tablespoons water (optional)
$\frac{1}{2}$ egg whites

Makes about $1\frac{1}{2}$ quarts.

Method
Put the sugar, lemon rind and water in a pan and heat until the sugar dissolves. Bring to a boil and simmer 4 minutes. Strain into the lemon juice.

If freezing the sherbet in ice trays, sprinkle the gelatin over 2 tablespoons water, let stand 5 minutes until spongy, then dissolve it over a pan of hot water and stir into the lemon mixture.

Cut the pineapple in half lengthwise, cut out the flesh with a grapefruit knife and discard the core; reserve the shells.

With a fork break the pineapple flesh into shreds and measure it — there should be 2–$2\frac{1}{2}$ cups. Add the flesh to the lemon mixture, taste for sweetness and chill.

Freeze the mixture in a churn freezer or ice tray. When slushy, stiffly beat the egg white and add 1 tablespoon to the sherbet. Continue freezing until it is firm.

To serve, chill the pineapple shells. Spread the strawberries or raspberries in the shells, and sprinkle with a little sugar. Shape the pineapple sherbet into balls with a scoop and pile on the fruit so some fruit is left showing. Arrange the pineapple halves on a silver platter lined with strawberry or vine leaves and serve.

Strawberry Sherbet

1 quart fresh strawberries
2–3 tablespoons confectioners' sugar
1 tablespoon kirsch (optional)
1 envelope gelatin and
$\quad \frac{1}{4}$ cup water (optional)
$\frac{1}{2}$ egg white

For sugar syrup
$\frac{3}{4}$ cup sugar
1 cup water

Makes about 1 quart.

Method
To make the sugar syrup: heat the sugar in the water until it is dissolved over low heat, then bring it to a boil and boil for 4 minutes. Let the syrup cool.

Hull the strawberries and work them through a sieve or purée in a blender; beat in the confectioners' sugar. Gradually stir the cold sugar syrup into the purée, add the kirsch, if you like, and taste for sweetness.

If freezing the sherbet in ice trays, sprinkle the gelatin over $\frac{1}{4}$ cup water, let stand 5 minutes or until spongy, dissolve it over a pan of hot water and stir in the strawberry mixture.

Chill the mixture and freeze in a churn freezer or ice trays. When slushy, stiffly beat the egg white and add 1 tablespoon to the sherbet. Continue freezing until it is firm.

Raspberry Sherbet

Follow the recipe for strawberry sherbet, substituting 1 quart raspberries for the strawberries. If puréeing in a blender, strain the purée to remove the seeds.

Sherry Sherbet

1 cup sherry
1 cup sugar
2 cups water
1 envelope gelatin
$\frac{1}{4}$ cup orange juice
$\frac{1}{2}$ cup lemon juice
pinch of salt
green food coloring (optional)
1 egg white

Makes about 1 quart.

Method
To make the sugar syrup: heat the sugar with the water until it is dissolved over low heat, bring to a boil and boil steadily until the syrup forms a thread between finger and thumb when a little is lifted on a spoon (230°F–234°F on a sugar thermometer). Take it from the heat and let cool slightly.

Sprinkle the gelatin over the orange juice and let stand 5 minutes until spongy and stir into the warm syrup until it is dissolved. Add the lemon juice and salt to the mixture, stir well and add the sherry. Stir in a few drops of green food coloring, if you like, and taste for sweetness.

Chill the mixture, freeze in a churn freezer or in ice trays. When slushy, stiffly beat the egg white and add 2 tablespoons to the sherbet. Continue freezing until it is firm.

For a spectacular dessert, serve orange sherbet (recipe is on page 109) — here the sherbet is molded in melon halves

Ice cream, sherbet and ices

Grapefruit with mint sherbet is topped with crystallized mint leaves (recipe is on page 112)

111

Grapefruit with Mint Sherbet

3 grapefruits
1 packed cup mint leaves,
    removed from stems
peeled rind of 2 lemons
$\frac{1}{2}$ cup sugar
2 cups water
$\frac{1}{3}$ cup lemon juice
2–3 drops of green food
    coloring (optional)
$\frac{1}{2}$ envelope gelatin and
    2 tablespoons water
    (optional)
$\frac{1}{2}$ egg white

For decoration
sugar
1 tablespoon chopped mint or
    8–10 crystallized mint leaves

Makes about $1\frac{1}{2}$ quarts.

Method

Put the sugar, lemon rind and water in a pan and heat gently until the sugar dissolves. Bring to a boil and simmer 4 minutes. Take from heat, add mint leaves and lemon juice, cover and leave to infuse over very low heat for 10–12 minutes.
Watchpoint: do not let mixture boil or the flavor will be bitter.

Strain the lemon mixture into a bowl, taste for sweetness, and add a few drops of green food coloring, if you like.

If freezing the sherbet in ice trays, sprinkle the gelatin over 2 tablespoons water, let stand 5 minutes and stir into the hot mixture until it dissolves.

Chill, then freeze the mixture in a churn freezer or ice trays. When slushy, stiffly beat the egg white and add 1 tablespoon to sherbet. Continue freezing until it is firm.

To prepare the grapefruit: cut each one in half and, using a grapefruit knife, remove the cores, then cut around the edges of the grapefruits between the flesh and the pith so the flesh is completely detached from the shells. Slip the knife down each side of the membrane dividing the grapefruit sections, then lift out all the membranes in one piece.

Remove any seeds and hollow out the centers enough to hold a scoop of sherbet, sprinkle with sugar and chill.

To serve: put a scoop of sherbet in the hollowed-out center of each grapefruit and sprinkle with a little chopped mint or add 2–3 crystallized mint leaves.

Crystallized Mint Leaves

Brush very fresh mint leaves with egg white, beaten until frothy. Sprinkle generously with sugar and place them on wax paper or on a wire rack in a cool airy place to dry for 1–2 hours. Use the leaves within 12 hours.

ICES, FRAPPES & GRANITES

Ices resemble sherbet as they are made from similar mixtures and are frozen by the same methods but contain no stabilizer. Lack of stabilizer gives an ice a firmer, coarser consistency than a sherbet. Ices can be frozen in ice trays but the texture is best when made in a churn freezer. Ices should be used within 24 hours as they will harden on standing.

Frappés are like ices but they must be frozen in ice trays and the mixture is stirred less during freezing so the finished frappé is granular; often small pieces of fruit are added to the basic mixture.

Frappés are usually served in sherbet glasses, often topped with whipped cream, or the frappé mixture may be added to bowls of cold punch to give texture. Do not store frappés for more than 24 hours as they harden to a solid mass.

Granités are very like frappés but the mixture is not stirred during freezing, so the consistency is very coarse, almost like rock salt. They must be frozen in ice cube trays.

Ices, frappés and granités should not be stored for more than 24 hours, as they will harden if kept any longer.

Lime Ice

1 cup lime juice
$1\frac{1}{3}$ cups sugar
4 cups cold water
few drops of green food
    coloring (optional)
8–10 crystallized mint leaves
    (see box)

Makes about $1\frac{1}{2}$ quarts.

Method

Heat the sugar with the water over low heat until dissolved, bring to a boil and simmer 8 minutes. Cool, add the lime juice, a few drops of coloring, if you like, and taste for sweetness; chill.

Freeze the mixture in a churn freezer or in ice trays until firm. Cover tightly and store in the freezer.

To serve, pile the ice in chilled sherbet glasses and top each one with crystallized mint leaves.

Champagne Ice

2 cups chilled Champagne
$\frac{3}{4}$ cup sugar
1 cup water
grated rind of $\frac{1}{2}$ orange
$\frac{1}{3}$ cup lemon juice
$\frac{1}{2}$ cup orange juice
pinch of salt

To finish
$1\frac{1}{2}$ tablespoons brandy,
    chilled
$\frac{1}{2}$ cup Champagne, chilled

Makes about 1 quart.

Method

To make the sugar syrup: heat the sugar with the water until dissolved, then bring to a boil and boil steadily until the syrup forms a thread between finger and thumb when a little is lifted on a spoon (230°F–234°F on a sugar thermometer). Let cool. Add the orange rind, both fruit juices and salt; chill and strain.

Stir in the chilled Champagne and freeze the mixture in a churn freezer or ice trays until firm. Cover tightly and store in the freezer.

To serve, mix the chilled brandy and Champagne, stir into the Champagne ice, pile in chilled sherbet glasses and serve at once.

Cranberry Frappé

1 quart cranberries
$\frac{1}{2}$ cup water
2 cups sugar
juice of 1 lemon
grated rind of 1 orange

Makes about 1 quart.

Method
Pick over cranberries, put them in a pan with $\frac{1}{2}$ cup water, cover and cook gently for 5 minutes or until very soft. Work them through a sieve and stir in the sugar until it is dissolved. Add the lemon juice and grated orange rind, taste for sweetness and chill.

Freeze the mixture in ice trays until the mixture has a rough texture, stirring several times. Cover it tightly and store in the freezer.

Raspberry Frappé

Make as for cranberry frappé, substituting 1 quart raspberries for the cranberries.

Strawberry Frappé

Make as for cranberry frappé, substituting 1 quart hulled strawberries for the cranberries.

Peach Frappé

6 ripe peaches
1$\frac{1}{2}$ cups sugar
1 cup water
$\frac{1}{4}$ teaspoon almond extract

Makes about 1 quart.

Method
Heat the sugar gently with the water until it is dissolved, then bring to a boil and boil until the mixture forms a thread between finger and thumb when a little is lifted on a spoon (230°F–234°F on a sugar thermometer). Let stand until cool.

Scald, peel and pit the peaches and crush them thoroughly or purée them in a blender. Stir in the sugar syrup and almond extract and chill.

Freeze the mixture in ice trays until the mixture has a rough texture, stirring several times. Cover it tightly and store in the freezer.

Coffee Cream Frappé

4 cups strong hot coffee
1 cup sugar
1 cup heavy cream
$\frac{1}{2}$ cup heavy cream, stiffly whipped (for serving)

Makes about 1$\frac{1}{2}$ quarts.

Method
Stir the sugar into the hot coffee until it is dissolved and let stand until cool. Stir in the heavy cream and chill.

Freeze the mixture in ice trays until the mixture has a rough texture, stirring several times. Cover it tightly and store in the freezer.

Top each serving with a spoonful of whipped cream.

Grapefruit Granité

2$\frac{1}{2}$ cups unsweetened grapefruit juice
2$\frac{1}{2}$ cups sugar
peeled rind of 1 orange
$\frac{2}{3}$ cup orange juice
peeled rind and juice of $\frac{1}{2}$ lemon
2 cups water
1 tablespoon rum
maraschino cherries (for decoration) – optional

Makes about 1$\frac{1}{2}$ quarts.

Method
Combine sugar, orange and lemon rinds and water in a pan and heat until the sugar is dissolved. Bring to a boil and simmer 4 minutes. Strain and cool. When cold add grapefruit, orange and lemon juices and rum. Taste for sweetness and chill.

Freeze in ice trays until firm and granular; then stir to break up the mixture.

To serve, pile in chilled sherbet glasses and top each one with a maraschino cherry, if you like.

Coffee Granité

2 cups hot espresso coffee
$\frac{1}{2}$ cup sugar
2 teaspoons vanilla extract
$\frac{1}{2}$ cup Chantilly cream (made with $\frac{1}{4}$ cup heavy cream, $\frac{1}{2}$ tablespoon sugar and a few drops of vanilla extract)

Makes about 2 cups.

Method
Dissolve the sugar in the coffee and stir in the vanilla. Freeze the mixture in ice trays until firm and granular, then stir to break up the mixture.

To serve, pile the granité in chilled sherbet glasses, and top each one with a little Chantilly cream.

113

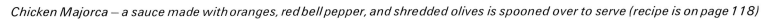

Chicken Majorca — a sauce made with oranges, red bell pepper, and shredded olives is spooned over to serve (recipe is on page 118)

SERVE CHICKEN WITH A SPANISH TOUCH

Sole Georgette
or
Cauliflower Soufflé
with Mornay Sauce

Chicken Majorca
Saffron Rice

Le Poirat
(Normandy Pear Tart)
or
Iced Strawberry Mousse

∾

Red wine – Valdepeñas (Spain)
or Gamay Beaujolais (California)

This menu uses simple ingredients in unusual ways. Stuff sole in a baked potato or purée cauliflower for a soufflé; combine chicken with orange and red pepper in an exotic entrée, and for dessert, cover fresh pears with a nutty cinnamon-flavored pastry or serve a mouth-watering iced strawberry mousse.

From the region of the legendary Don Quixote comes a red wine well suited to the Spanish-style entrée. Valdepeñas is a fruity, refreshing wine with plenty of character despite its light color and body. Indeed, it might well be thought of as a robust rosé, easy on the palate yet with enough individuality to match the seasonings of the chicken. A worthy competitor is a California Gamay Beaujolais. Both wines will be improved by 15 minutes in the refrigerator before they are served.

TIMETABLE

Morning
Prepare the pastry dough and chill 1 hour.
Scrub the potatoes, roll them in salt, prick and bake. Cook the fish, make sauce, complete sole Georgette ready for reheating and refrigerate.
Prepare soufflé dish. Make soufflé mixture but do not add egg whites. Infuse milk for mornay sauce.
Cut chicken into pieces; prepare the red pepper, orange and olives.
Soak the saffron; cook rice, drain and store in covered container. Cook onion for rice and let stand in the pan. Roll out the pastry dough and line the flan ring or springform pan. Pare and quarter pears; fill, cover and bake pie.
Make strawberry purée for mousse; make the mousse, pour into dishes or glasses, cover and freeze.

Assemble ingredients for final cooking from 7 p.m. for dinner around 8 p.m.

You will find that **cooking times** given in the individual recipes for these dishes have sometimes been adapted in the timetable to help you when cooking and serving this menu as a party meal.

Order of Work

7:00
Start cooking chicken; leave to simmer on top of stove if you have only one oven.

7:15
Set oven at moderate (350°F) for sole *or hot (425°F) for soufflé.*
Make mornay sauce but do not add cheese; keep warm in a water bath.

7:25
Whip cream for pear pie and chill.

7:35
Reheat sole Georgette.
Beat egg whites for soufflé; heat cauliflower mixture until lukewarm, fold in egg whites and bake soufflé.

7:45
Heat the rice and the saffron in pan with onion and butter.
If making soufflé, reheat rice in a hot oven later.
Complete chicken and keep warm.
Add cheese to mornay sauce.

8:00
Serve sole *or soufflé. If serving soufflé,* put rice in hot oven to reheat for 10 minutes.
If serving pear pie warm, turn oven to very low (200°F) and put in pie after rice has been reheated. Spoon cream into center of pie just before serving.

Appetizer

Sole Georgette

2 medium fillets of sole
(1–1¼ lb)
4 large baking potatoes
salt and pepper
½ cup white wine
¼ cup water
slice of onion
6 peppercorns
1½ tablespoons butter
1 tablespoon flour
6 tablespoons light cream
½ cup (¼ lb) cooked, peeled shrimps, coarsely chopped

To finish
2 tablespoons light cream
2 tablespoons butter
¼ cup grated Parmesan cheese (for sprinkling)

Pastry bag and large star tube

Method
Set oven at moderate (350°F).
Scrub the potatoes well, dry them with paper towels, roll them in salt and prick with a fork. Bake in the heated oven for 1¼–1½ hours or until tender.
Wash the fillets of sole and pat them dry with paper towels; cut each fillet in half lengthwise and fold in half to the same length as the potatoes.
Put the fillets in an ovenproof dish, add the wine and water, onion and peppercorns and cover with foil or a lid. Poach the fish for 10–12 minutes or until it flakes easily when tested with a fork. Drain fillets on paper towels, reserving the liquid.
Melt the butter in a saucepan, stir in the flour until smooth and strain in the reserved fish liquid. Season and bring to a boil, stirring constantly. Simmer 2 minutes,

take from the heat, stir in the 6 tablespoons light cream and adjust the seasoning. Mix a little sauce with the shrimps to bind them.
When the baked potatoes can be pierced easily with a fork, cut off the tops lengthwise, scoop out the pulp and spread the shrimp mixture in the potato shells. Lay a fillet of sole on top and coat the fish with remaining sauce.
Increase oven heat to hot (400°F).
Mash the potato pulp and beat in the light cream with butter and seasoning. Spoon this purée into a pastry bag fitted with a star tube and pipe a border around the edge of each filled potato. Sprinkle with Parmesan cheese and bake in the heated oven for 10 minutes or until the potato is golden brown. Alternatively, replace the potato lid instead of making the potato border and heat for a few minutes in the oven.
If preparing this dish in advance and refrigerating, reheat for 20–25 minutes in a moderate oven (350°F) so the filling is thoroughly heated.
Serve the potatoes very hot in a napkin.

After baking potatoes, scoop the pulp from the skins and fill shells with the fish mixture

Pipe a border of potato purée around edge of filled potatoes and sprinkle with cheese

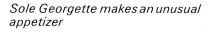

Sole Georgette makes an unusual appetizer

Alternative
appetizer

Cauliflower Soufflé
with Mornay Sauce

1 medium cauliflower
2 tablespoons browned
   breadcrumbs
1 bay leaf
béchamel sauce, made with
   3 tablespoons butter,
   2½ tablespoons flour, 1 cup
   milk (infused with slice of
   onion, 6 peppercorns,
   blade of mace and bay leaf)
salt and pepper
4 egg yolks
5–6 egg whites
1 tablespoon grated Parmesan
   cheese (for sprinkling)

For mornay sauce
2 tablespoons butter
2 tablespoons flour
1½ cups milk (infused as for
   béchamel sauce)
½ cup grated cheese (half
   Parmesan and half Gruyère)

Soufflé dish (1½ quart capacity)

Method
Set oven at hot (425°F). Butter the dish and sprinkle with browned breadcrumbs. Tie a foil or wax paper collar around the dish to allow for expansion of the soufflé mixture.

Cut the cauliflower in quarters and discard the hard core. Cook it in plenty of boiling salted water, with the bay leaf, for 8–10 minutes or until the cauliflower is quite tender when pierced with a fork. Drain it well, refresh and drain again. Work the quarters through a sieve.

Prepare the béchamel sauce and stir into the cauliflower purée. Alternatively, work the béchamel sauce with the drained cauliflower quarters in a blender. Season well.

Beat the egg yolks into the cauliflower mixture, one at a time; reheat the mixture until warm to the touch. Beat the egg whites until they hold a stiff peak and fold one-quarter of them into the warm cauliflower mixture with a large metal spoon. Add the remaining egg whites and fold together as lightly as possible.

Pour the mixture into the prepared dish and sprinkle with the grated cheese. Bake the soufflé in the heated oven for 15–20 minutes or until it is well risen and brown.

Prepare mornay sauce while the soufflé is baking and keep hot.

Remove the paper collar from the soufflé and serve at once; serve mornay sauce separately.

Entrée

Chicken Majorca

3½–4 lb roasting chicken
2 tablespoons olive oil
1 tablespoon butter
1 medium onion, thinly sliced
2 teaspoons flour
½ cup well-flavored stock
   (made from chicken giblets)
½ cup white wine
salt and pepper
bouquet garni (including a strip
   of orange peel)
1 red bell pepper
1 large orange, peeled and
   thinly sliced
6 large green olives,
   pitted and shredded
1 tablespoon chopped parsley

Method
Cut the chicken into serving pieces.

In a large frying pan or skillet, heat the oil and butter and, when foaming, put in chicken pieces, skin side down. Sauté the pieces over medium heat until golden brown on both sides. Remove the pieces, add the onion and cook until just golden.

Stir in the flour until smooth, add the stock and wine and bring to a boil, stirring. Season, return the chicken pieces to the pan and add bouquet garni.

Cover and simmer the chicken pieces on top of the stove or in a moderate oven (350°F) for 25–30 minutes or until tender when tested with a skewer. Remove the bouquet garni.

Broil the red pepper or hold it over a flame until the thin skin is charred all over. Using a knife, peel off the skin and rinse pepper under running water if necessary. Core the pepper, discard the seeds and cut into strips.

To serve, arrange the chicken pieces in a warm serving dish. Add the red pepper strips, orange slices, olive shreds and chopped parsley to the sauce. Bring just to a boil, taste for seasoning and spoon over the chicken. Serve with saffron rice.

Chicken Stock

When cooking a whole chicken, make stock from the giblets (neck, gizzard, heart and feet, if available); never add the liver because it gives a bitter flavor. (The liver is better for making pâté or sautéed for a snack.)

Heat a thick saucepan with scarcely enough fat to cover the base; then add the giblets and an onion, halved and washed but not peeled, and 'dry fry' over a high heat until lightly browned. Remove the pan from the heat and add 1 quart cold water. Add ¼ teaspoon salt, a few peppercorns, and a bouquet garni. Cover and simmer gently for 1–2 hours. Strain.

Put browned chicken pieces back into the pan with the bouquet garni after making sauce

Peel the charred skin from the red bell pepper before discarding the core and seeds

Accompaniment to entrée

Saffron Rice

1 cup rice
pinch of saffron, soaked for 30 minutes in 2 tablespoons boiling water
2 tablespoons butter
1 small onion, thinly sliced
salt and pepper

Method

Cook the rice in plenty of boiling salted water for about 12 minutes or until tender. Drain it in a colander, rinse with hot water and let rice stand until thoroughly drained.

Melt the butter in a frying pan, add the onion and cook slowly until golden brown. Stir in the rice and add the saffron liquid. With a fork, toss the rice over heat, adding more butter if necessary to make a rich but fluffy mixture. Season with salt and pepper.

Le poirat (Normandy pear pie) is served with whipped cream in the center

Dessert

Le Poirat
(Normandy Pear Pie)

2–3 firm Anjou or Bosc pears
granulated sugar
(for sprinkling)
½ cup heavy cream

For pastry
2 cups flour
2 teaspoons ground cinnamon
½ cup chopped walnuts, ground
10 tablespoons butter
½ cup sugar
1 egg
½ teaspoon vanilla
1½ tablespoons water

*8–9 inch flan ring or springform
pan; 2½ inch cookie cutter*

This pie is a specialty of the French province of Normandy, famous for its excellent fruit and cream.

Method
To make the pastry dough: sift the flour with cinnamon onto a board or marble slab and add the walnuts. Make a well in the center, add the butter, sugar, egg, vanilla and water and work together with the fingertips until smooth. Gradually draw in the flour mixture, working with the whole hand to form a smooth dough. Wrap in plastic wrap or foil and chill 1 hour.

Set oven at hot (400°F).

Roll out about two-thirds of the dough on a lightly floured board and line the flan ring or pan. Roll out the remaining dough and cut it in a circle large enough to cover the top of the pie; cut a 2½ inch circle in the center of this lid.

Pare, core and quarter the pears. Arrange the pear quarters in the dough-lined pan, with the thin ends of the pears meeting in the center. Cover with the dough circle, press the dough edges together to seal them, brush with a little water and sprinkle generously with sugar. Bake the pie in the heated oven for 15 minutes, turn down the oven heat to moderate (350°F) and bake 25–30 minutes longer or until the pears are tender when pierced with a skewer.

Whip the cream until it holds a soft shape and just before serving, spoon it into the center opening of the pie. Serve pie warm or cold.

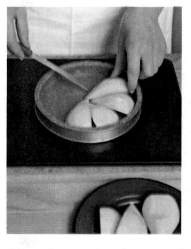

Place the pared and quartered pears in the dough-lined pan, thin ends towards the center

Using a rolling pin, cover the pears with a circle of dough and press the edges together

Alternative dessert

Iced Strawberry Mousse

3 cups fresh strawberries, hulled, or 3 cups frozen strawberries without sugar, thawed
½ cup sugar
⅓ cup water
2 egg whites
¾ cup heavy cream, whipped until it holds a soft shape
2 tablespoons finely chopped browned almonds (for garnish)
4 small fresh strawberries (for garnish) – optional

4 individual soufflé dishes or parfait glasses

Method
If using soufflé dishes, tie paper collars around them to extend 1½ inches above the edge of the dish.

Purée fresh or frozen strawberries in a blender or work them through a food mill — there should be about 1½ cups purée.

Heat the sugar with the water until the sugar is dissolved. Bring to a boil and boil until the syrup forms a thread between finger and thumb when a little is lifted on a spoon (230°F–234°F on a sugar thermometer).

Meanwhile stiffly whip the egg whites. Pour the hot sugar syrup gradually into the egg whites, beating constantly, and continue beating until the meringue is cool and very stiff.

Fold in the strawberry purée, followed by the lightly whipped cream, and pour the mixture into the prepared soufflé dishes or parfait glasses. Freeze at least 4 hours or until firm. If making ahead, cover the mousse tightly and store up to 2 months in the freezer.

To serve: peel the paper carefully from the soufflé dishes, if used, and press chopped browned almonds around the edge; if using parfait glasses, sprinkle almonds on top of the mousse. Top each mousse with a small fresh strawberry, if you like, and serve while still frozen.

Schwäbisches Reh, a roasted leg of venison served with traditional accompaniments, is a German delicacy (recipe is on page 132)

GERMAN COOKING

German food has a direct appeal — the cooking is hearty, wholesome and full of flavor. Steaming meaty soups, chewy dark rye bread, cabbage in innumerable guises, savory sausages, plump dumplings and rich, mouth-watering cakes are typical of Germany; and within such broad outlines lies a wealth of dishes that vary greatly from region to region. The recipes on the following pages give a taste of the robust dishes characteristic of German cooking.

Regional Specialties

In the north, near the sea, the food resembles that of Scandinavia with fish, particularly herring, as a dominant ingredient, and plenty of pickled meats and root vegetables like beets; fruits are made into compotes or served in sweet and sour combinations with meat. To the east, the Slavic influence shows in a love of sour cream, paprika and caraway. This is the home, too, of the dumpling — produced in a multitude of savory, sweet light or substantial combinations.

The west is wine country, where Germany's finest vintages are produced in the Rhine valley. Here the food is lighter and not as highly spiced. The famous Himmel und Erde (heaven and earth) — a mixture of potato and apple purée, generally served with sausages, comes from the Rhine, as does a gentle Sauerbraten whose usual vinegary taste is softened by sugar and cake or cookie crumbs.

Most familiar to North Americans is the cooking of Bavaria, in southern Germany. Cabbage, beer, and sausages are particularly Bavarian, and many towns have their 'own' sausages that other parts of Germany have adopted.

Wursts (sausages) come in all shapes and sizes. They range from Thuringer Blutwurst (made with lean pork and blood), to Stuttgarter Presskopf (pork, veal and beef). The delicate Weisswurst, made of veal speckled with parsley, was invented in Munich and Nuremberg claims particular credit for its Bratwurst, a mixture of coarsely ground pork and spices.

The Germans have an unerring knack for picking the richest ingredients for their choicest dishes. Among meats, pork is a favorite, as is goose among poultry, and herring, eel and salmon among fish.

One German specialty is rare here — game. Bavaria, the Black Forest, and eastern Germany still boast plentiful supplies of large game including boar, deer, game birds and ground game like rabbit. Venison haunch or saddle, roast or braised in red wine and served with cranberry sauce and wild mushrooms, and partridge stuffed with green grapes and sauced with sour cream, are both party dishes, but rabbit is a popular everyday dinner, often stewed and served with red cabbage.

German cakes (Torten) and pastries need no introduction; butter, eggs, nuts and cream are not stinted in creating the superbly rich layer cakes, spicy crisp cookies, and huge variety of yeast breads and coffeecakes eaten as mid-morning and afternoon snacks.

German appetites match the heartiness of the cooking. The day begins with a light breakfast of coffee and rolls, followed by a mid-morning sandwich of cheese or sausage or perhaps more coffee and pastry.

Lunch is traditionally the main meal of the day with two or three courses, although in large cities during the week many people eat the main meal at night.

Late afternoon finds Germans repeating the morning snack, and supper usually consists of cold meats, smoked or pickled fish or cheese, with a nourishing soup or a rich dessert.

German Drinks

Drinks in Germany are just as important — and copious — as the food. Beer is universally popular and there are many kinds, some available nationwide, others offered by the local brewery.

White wines from the Rhine with its tributary river, the Moselle, and Bocksbeutel in its characteristic flat bottle, vie with and even surpass beer in the grape-growing areas.

For those with stronger tastes, the Germans fire their palates with Schnaps. Like the Scandinavian version, this German spirit is distilled from grain or potatoes and flavored with juniper. Schnaps chased with beer and vice versa is the habit when eating sausages or herring.

Geflügelklein-suppe
(Giblet Soup)

2 lb chicken, duck, goose or turkey giblets
3 quarts water
3 slices of bacon, diced
1 onion, diced
1 carrot, diced
2 stalks of celery, diced
$\frac{1}{2}$ cup pearl barley
$\frac{1}{4}$ teaspoon grated nutmeg
salt and pepper
1 tablespoon chopped parsley (for serving)

Method

Wash the giblets thoroughly (do not use the liver as this makes the soup bitter). Put the giblets in a pan with the water, cover and simmer $1\frac{1}{2}$ hours, skimming off any scum that rises to the surface. Strain the stock and reserve it.

Chop the giblets finely and pull the meat from the neck, discarding the bones.

In a kettle fry the bacon until soft, add the onion, carrot and celery and continue cooking until the vegetables are soft but not browned.

Pour in the reserved stock, add the giblet meat and pearl barley with nutmeg and seasoning and simmer, uncovered, for 30 minutes or until the barley is tender and the soup is reduced and well flavored.

Taste the soup for seasoning and sprinkle a little parsley over each bowl before serving.

Biersuppe
(Hot Beer Soup)

1 quart light beer
$\frac{1}{4}$ cup sugar
peeled rind of 1 lemon
6 whole cloves
3 inch piece of cinnamon stick
2 teaspoons cornstarch, mixed
    to a paste with 2 tablespoons
    water
2 egg yolks, beaten to mix
salt and pepper
snow dumplings (for garnish)

Method
Let the beer stand for 1 hour or until the bubbles have subsided. Put the beer in a kettle with the sugar, lemon rind, cloves and cinnamon, tied in a piece of cheesecloth, and heat gently until the sugar dissolves. Bring the mixture just to a boil, cover and let infuse over low heat for 15 minutes; discard the cheesecloth bag.

Stir the cornstarch paste into the hot soup and heat gently, stirring, until the soup thickens. Simmer 2 minutes, take from the heat and stir a little of the hot soup into the egg yolks. Stir this mixture back into the remaining soup, taste for seasoning and serve with 2–3 snow dumplings floating in each bowl.

Blue trout is a popular dish anywhere in Germany where fresh trout from local streams are available. Ideally, the trout should be brought live to the kitchen as the distinctive blue color is lost if they are killed more than 15 minutes before cooking.

Eel can also be cooked in the same way.

Bierkaltschale
(Cold Beer Soup)

1 quart light beer
$\frac{3}{4}$ cup currants
2 slices of pumpernickel bread
$\frac{1}{2}$ cup sugar (or to taste)
$\frac{1}{2}$ teaspoon ground cinnamon
$\frac{1}{2}$ teaspoon ground cloves
juice of $\frac{1}{2}$ lemon
snow dumplings or 1 lemon,
    thinly sliced (for garnish)

Method
Pour boiling water over the currants, let stand 30 minutes until they are plump, then drain them.

Cut the pumpernickel bread into cubes and work it into fine crumbs in a blender or rub it through a wire sieve.

Add the currants, pumpernickel crumbs, sugar, spices and lemon juice to the beer, stir well, cover and chill, stirring occasionally.

When the mixture is very cold, add more sugar or spices to taste and serve the soup with snow dumplings or lemon slices floating on top.

Schrecklösschen
(Snow Dumplings)

Bring a pan of water to a boil. Beat 2 egg whites until they hold a stiff peak and beat in 1 tablespoon sugar until the mixture is glossy. Fold in 2 more tablespoons sugar and drop teaspoonsful of the mixture into simmering water.

Cover the pan, take from the heat and leave in a warm place for 8–10 minutes or until the dumplings are swollen and firm to the touch.

Lift the dumplings out with a slotted spoon and drain on paper towels. Serve with beer or fruit soups.

Forelle-blau
(Blue Trout)

4 live trout (each $\frac{3}{4}$–1 lb)
$\frac{1}{4}$ cup white wine vinegar
$\frac{1}{4}$ cup white wine
1 quart water
2 small white onions, sliced
6 peppercorns
salt

For garnish
$\frac{1}{2}$ cup melted butter
1 tablespoon chopped parsley
1 lemon, cut in wedges

Method
Stun the trout with a blow on the head. Clean them, working through the gills instead of slitting the stomach. Wash the stomach cavity thoroughly; do not scrape off the scales as these, when cooked in vinegar, give the trout the blue color. Trim the tails and tie each head to the tail with string so they form a circle.

In a shallow pan bring the vinegar, wine and water to a boil with the onions, peppercorns and a little salt. Simmer 2 minutes, add the trout (the liquid should cover them), cover the pan and bring just back to a boil. Take from the heat and let stand 10–12 minutes — the fish are cooked when a fin can be pulled out easily.

Drain the trout, remove the string, arrange them on a platter and garnish with chopped parsley and lemon wedges. Serve the trout with melted butter and boiled small new potatoes sprinkled with parsley.

Kartoffelpuffer
(Potato Pancakes)

7 medium potatoes, peeled
1 egg, beaten to mix
2 teaspoons flour
salt and pepper
bacon fat or lard (for frying)

Potato pancakes are often served as a separate course after soup or sausages and they may have a grated onion added to the mixture for flavor. Alternatively, they may be a dessert, served with apple sauce or cranberry compote.

If hot, they must be served at once because they lose crispness quickly, but they can also be sprinkled with sugar to eat cold with coffee. Makes about 12 pancakes.

Method
Grate the potatoes onto a piece of cheesecloth and squeeze them tightly, catching the liquid in a bowl. Let stand a few minutes for the starch to settle, then pour off the liquid and add the grated potato to the starch remaining in the bowl. Stir in the beaten egg, flour and seasoning.

Watchpoint: grated potatoes discolor so work as fast as possible.

Pour a $\frac{1}{2}$ inch layer of melted bacon fat or lard into a skillet and heat until it sputters when a drop of water is added. Add the potato mixture in $\frac{1}{4}$ cup quantities and flatten slightly with a spatula. Fry the pancakes about 2 minutes until golden brown, turn them and brown on the other side. Drain the pancakes on paper towels and keep hot while frying the remaining mixture.

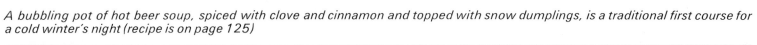

A bubbling pot of hot beer soup, spiced with clove and cinnamon and topped with snow dumplings, is a traditional first course for a cold winter's night (recipe is on page 125)

Dumplings

Dumplings are a German as well as a Central European favorite.

Potato dumplings may be made with raw or cooked potatoes and are sometimes stuffed with a fried bread croûton or sprinkled with fried breadcrumbs. They are served with meat dishes, preferably with a gravy. **Bread dumplings** often contain meat. Some bread dumplings are added to soups; others, like Königsberger Klopse, with a high proportion of meat, are served as an entrée with a sauce or used to garnish meat dishes.

Fish and liver dumplings are popular variations served either in soups or as an entrée.

Sweet dumplings include yeast dumplings that are usually served with a fruit or vanilla custard sauce, cottage cheese dumplings, dumplings stuffed with plums or apricots and topped with breadcrumbs fried in butter, and meringue (snow) dumplings (see page 125) added as a garnish for fruit and beer soups.

Potato Dumplings

4 medium potatoes
1 slice of bread, crusts removed
1–2 tablespoons butter
large pinch of ground mace
1 small egg, beaten to mix
$\frac{1}{2}$ cup flour
1 tablespoon cornstarch
salt and pepper
3–4 tablespoons melted butter (for serving)

Makes 18–20 dumplings.

Method
Wash the potatoes and cook them, unpeeled, in boiling salted water for 15–20 minutes or until they are tender. Drain them, peel and work them through a sieve or mash them until smooth. Let cool.

Cut the bread in cubes. In a pan heat the butter, add the cubes of bread and fry them until they are golden brown. Drain them on paper towels.

Add the mace, egg, flour, cornstarch and seasoning to the potato. Mix well and shape the mixture into balls $1\frac{1}{2}$ inches in diameter. Press 2 cubes of fried bread into the middle of each dumpling, making sure the potato covers the bread completely.

Put the dumplings in a large pan of boiling salted water, taking care not to fill the pan too full – there should be only 1 layer of potato dumplings at a time. Simmer, uncovered, for 12–15 minutes, turning them occasionally. Drain well. Serve hot with melted butter poured over.

Königsberger Klopse
(Meat Dumplings)

$\frac{3}{4}$ lb ground pork
$\frac{3}{4}$ lb ground beef or veal
2 dry hamburger buns, soaked in water and squeezed dry
1 tablespoon butter
2 onions, quartered
4 anchovy fillets
1 tablespoon chopped parsley
salt
black pepper, freshly ground
2 eggs, beaten to mix
3 cups stock

For sauce
2 tablespoons butter
2 tablespoons flour
juice of 1 lemon
2–3 tablespoons capers, drained

Method
In a skillet heat the butter and brown the onion quarters over medium heat. Work the onions with the ground meats, soaked buns and anchovy fillets through the fine blade of a grinder. Add the parsley with plenty of seasoning and stir in the beaten egg to bind the mixture.

Divide the mixture into even-sized portions, wet the palms of your hands, and roll the mixture into 2 inch balls.

Bring the stock to a boil in a shallow pan, add the dumplings, cover and simmer 20 minutes or until the dumplings rise to the surface. Lift them out with a slotted spoon, pile them into a serving dish and keep warm. Reserve the cooking liquid.

To make the sauce: melt the butter in a pan, stir in the flour and cook, stirring, until pale straw-colored. Strain in the cooking liquid from the dumplings and bring the sauce to a boil, stirring. Simmer until it is the consistency of heavy cream, then add the lemon juice and capers and taste for seasoning.

Spoon the sauce over the dumplings and serve them with boiled potatoes or sauerkraut.

Zwetschgen-knödel
(Plum Dumplings)

18–20 ripe Italian or prune plums
18–20 sugar cubes

For dough
4 medium potatoes, peeled
$\frac{1}{2}$ cup flour
1 tablespoon potato starch or cornstarch
pinch of salt
1 small egg, beaten to mix

To finish
$\frac{1}{2}$ cup butter
$\frac{3}{4}$ cup fresh white breadcrumbs
2–3 tablespoons sugar (for sprinkling)

These dumplings are equally good made with fresh apricots. Makes 18–20 dumplings.

Method
Pit the plums and press a sugar cube into the center of each plum.

To make the dough: cook the potatoes in boiling salted water for 15–20 minutes or until tender, drain and work them through a ricer or mash them until smooth. Let cool, add the flour, potato starch or cornstarch and salt. Make a well in the center, add the beaten egg and mix to a smooth dough as lightly as possible.

Roll out the dough on a floured board to $\frac{1}{4}$ inch thickness and cut into $2\frac{1}{2}$ inch squares. Set a plum in the center of each square and pinch and shape the dough around it to make a smooth ball.

Bring a shallow pan of water to a boil, drop in the dumplings and simmer 10–15 minutes or until the dough is cooked. Drain the dumplings, pile in a dish and keep warm.

To finish: melt the butter in a pan, add the breadcrumbs and fry until browned. Pour the breadcrumbs and butter over the dumplings, sprinkle with sugar and serve at once.

Eisbein mit Erbspurée
(Pork Hocks with Pea Purée)

4 lb fresh pork hocks, cut in
   2–3 inch pieces
1 onion, stuck with 2 cloves
1 bay leaf
6 whole allspice berries
6 peppercorns
salt

For pea purée
1 cup ($\frac{1}{2}$ lb) split yellow peas,
   soaked overnight and
   drained
1 onion, halved
bouquet garni
salt and pepper
4 slices of bacon, diced
1 onion sliced

For serving
cooked sauerkraut
boiled potatoes

This is a famous Berlin dish; it is often made with smoked pork hocks, but is equally good with fresh hocks.

Method
Put the pork hocks in a pan with water to cover, bring slowly to a boil and skim well. Add the onion, bay leaf, all-spice berries, peppercorns and salt, cover and simmer 2–2$\frac{1}{2}$ hours or until the meat is very tender and falls easily from the bones.

To make the pea purée: put the split peas in a pan with the halved onion, bouquet garni and water to cover. Add the lid, bring to a boil and simmer 1$\frac{1}{2}$–2 hours or until the peas are quite tender.

Drain them, discarding the onion and bouquet garni, reserve the liquid and work the peas through a strainer or food mill or purée them in a blender with a little of the liquid. Return them to the pan, add salt and pepper to taste with enough reserved cooking liquid to make a purée that falls fairly easily from the spoon. Reheat thoroughly.

Fry the bacon until soft, add the sliced onion and fry until the bacon and onion are browned; discard excess fat.

Pile the pea purée in a dish and scatter the onion and bacon mixture on top. Pile the sauerkraut on a platter, drain the pork hocks, set them on top and serve the pea purée and boiled potatoes separately.

Gekochtes Sauerkraut
(Cooked Sauerkraut)

4 cups (2 lb) fresh or canned
   sauerkraut
$\frac{1}{4}$ cup beef drippings, bacon fat
   or lard
2 onions, diced
2 tart apples, pared, cored and
   diced
1 bay leaf
6 juniper berries, crushed or
   1 teaspoon caraway seeds
1 teaspoon sugar
salt and pepper
2$\frac{1}{2}$–3 cups stock
1 medium potato, peeled

Fresh sauerkraut is available in some delicatessens.

Method
Drain fresh sauerkraut, cover with cold water and soak 15 minutes; drain thoroughly and press out the water with your hands. If using canned sauerkraut, rinse and drain it thoroughly. Tear the sauerkraut into shreds with your hands so it does not form lumps.

In a flameproof casserole (without a cast iron surface) melt the drippings, fat or lard and fry the onions and apples until soft but not browned. Add the sauerkraut, bay leaf, juniper berries or caraway seeds, sugar and a little seasoning and mix well. Cover the pot and cook gently for 5 minutes until the fat is absorbed.

Pour over enough stock almost to cover the sauerkraut, cover the pot and simmer gently on top of the stove for $\frac{3}{4}$ hour.

Grate the potato, stir into the pot and cook 10–15 minutes longer or until the sauerkraut is tender but still firm. The potato will disintegrate and thicken the mixture – if it is too thick, add a little more stock. Taste for seasoning before serving.

Bratwurst im Biersosse
(Bratwurst in Beer)

4 pairs (1–1$\frac{1}{2}$ lb) Bratwurst
2 cups light beer
2 tablespoons butter
1 onion, chopped
1 teaspoon sugar
$\frac{1}{2}$ cup dark rye breadcrumbs
salt and pepper

Method
Pour boiling water over the Bratwurst to cover them, simmer 5 minutes and drain.

In a skillet heat the butter and brown the Bratwurst on all sides. Take them out, add the onion and sugar and cook gently, stirring, until brown and the sugar has caramelized.

Pour in the beer, add the rye breadcrumbs and season-ing and put back the sausages. Cover the pan and simmer 20 minutes. Serve Bratwurst with boiled or mashed pota-toes.

Himmel und Erde
(Apple and Potato Purée)

4 medium potatoes, peeled
2 tart apples, pared, cored and
   sliced
1–2 tablespoons sugar
salt and pepper
$\frac{1}{4}$ cup butter
1 onion, sliced

The southern German word for potato – Erdapfel or earth apple – suggests the name for this dish of potato and apple purée, called Heaven and Earth. Serve with roast meats and sausages.

Method
Cook the potatoes in boiling salted water for 15–20 min-utes or until tender, drain and work them through a ricer or mash them.

Thickly butter a saucepan, add the apples and sugar to taste, cover and cook gently for 10–15 minutes, stirring occasionally, until the apples are pulpy. Stir apples into the mashed potatoes, season to taste and pile in a serving dish.

In a skillet heat the butter and fry the onion until browned. Pour the butter and fried onion over the potato mixture and serve.

Bratwurst is one of the most popular German sausages, available in many delicatessens and from some butchers. Made of coarsely ground pork, sometimes with veal added, it has a mildly spicy flavor. Recipes for other German sausages are given in Volume 12.

Rheinischer Sauerbraten
(Rhineland Marinated Beef)

3 lb rump or round steak
$\frac{1}{4}$ lb piece of bacon, cut in $\frac{1}{4}$ inch
   strips (for larding)
2 tablespoons oil
2 onions, sliced
2 stalks of celery, sliced
3 leeks, sliced (optional)
bouquet garni
salt and pepper
$\frac{1}{2}$ cup gingersnap crumbs or
   honey cake crumbs
pinch of sugar

For marinade
2 cups white wine vinegar
2 cups water
1 onion, sliced
1 carrot, sliced
1 bayleaf
2 tablespoons sugar
5 juniper berries, crushed
6 peppercorns

For garnish
2–3 tart apples
2 tablespoons butter
1 tablespoon sugar
$\frac{1}{4}$ cup slivered almonds,
   browned

Larding needle

Method

Lard the beef with the strips of bacon (see right).

Combine the ingredients for the marinade in a pan, bring to a boil and simmer 5 minutes. Cool, then pour over the beef in a deep bowl (not aluminum) so the beef is covered with marinade. Cover and keep in the refrigerator for 3–4 days, turning the meat from time to time. Drain the meat and pat dry with paper towels; strain the marinade and reserve.

In a flameproof casserole heat the oil, brown the beef on all sides and take out. Turn down the heat, add the sliced vegetables, cover and cook gently for 5–7 minutes or until they are soft.

Set the beef on top, add the bouquet garni and seasoning, and pour in enough strained marinade to reach halfway up the beef. Cover and simmer gently $2-2\frac{1}{2}$ hours or until the beef is very tender.

Transfer the beef to a platter and keep warm. Add the gingersnaps or cake crumbs to the pan and simmer 10 minutes or until the crumbs have disintegrated. Strain the sauce into a pan, pressing well so the crumbs and vegetables are puréed into the sauce. Bring to a boil, taste for seasoning, adding salt, pepper and a pinch of sugar, if necessary. Spoon a little sauce over the beef, and serve the rest separately.

To make the garnish: wipe and core the apples but do not pare them. Cut them in $\frac{3}{8}$ inch slices. In a skillet melt the butter, sprinkle the apple slices with sugar and fry them briskly in the butter, sugar side down. When browned and the sugar has caramelized, sprinkle the tops with sugar, turn them over and brown the other side.

Arrange the fried apple rings around the side of the dish, sprinkle the top with browned almonds and serve with potato dumplings (see page 127) or spätzle.

Larding

Larding means the insertion of small strips of fresh pork fat or bacon into the flesh of meat that has very little natural fat. This prevents meats such as fillet of beef, veal and venison from drying out when roasted.

The fat used must be white, firm and dry and cut into pieces about $\frac{1}{4}$ inch wide and $1\frac{1}{2}$ inches long. The fat should be chilled before it is cut into strips. It is threaded into a larding needle – a large needle with a channel to enclose the fat, or with a spring at the end to catch the fat so it can be pulled through the meat.

The strip is literally 'sewn' into the meat, leaving both ends hanging over the surface.

Larding is always done across the grain of the meat.

Spätzle

In a bowl put 3 cups flour with $\frac{1}{2}$ teaspoon salt and make a well in the center. Add 2 eggs, beaten to mix with 1 cup water, and work to form a smooth, soft dough, adding a little more flour or water if necessary.

Divide the dough in half and press out thinly on a floured board.

Have a large pan of boiling salted water ready. Cut thin slivers of dough with a knife (wet the knife to prevent the slivers from sticking) and drop them into the boiling water. Simmer gently for 5–7 minutes or until the Spätzle rise to the surface. Lift them out with a slotted spoon and keep in a warm place in a pan with 3–4 tablespoons melted butter.

Cook the remaining Spätzle in the same way, add them to the butter and heat thoroughly with plenty of pepper and a little salt if needed.

The Spätzle may be served while still tender and white or they may be fried in the butter until golden.

Sauerbraten, literally sour roast, means beef that is marinated in vinegar and wine to give a characteristic sharp flavor, then braised with vegetables and served with a rich sauce.

There are many recipes from all over Germany – the one here from the Rhineland is sweetened with gingersnaps; a tarter version of sauerbraten made with red wine was given in Volume 5.

A typical German favorite is Rinderrouladen – individual beef rolls braised in a rich brown sauce, and served with potato dumplings, red cabbage and a mug of beer

Rinderrouladen
(Beef Rolls)

$1\frac{1}{2}$–2 lb round steak, cut in
  8–10 thin slices
2 tablespoons oil
1 onion, chopped
bouquet garni
1 cup red wine
1 cup beef stock
salt and pepper

For filling
1–2 tablespoons prepared
  mustard
8–10 slices of bacon, chopped
1 onion, chopped
1 tablespoon chopped parsley
8–10 gherkin pickles or
  3 medium dill pickles,
  quartered lengthwise

For sauce
1 tablespoon butter
1 tablespoon flour
$\frac{1}{4}$ cup sour cream

Method
If the steak slices are not very thin, place them between 2 pieces of wax paper and pound with a mallet or rolling pin until they are $\frac{1}{4}$ inch thick.

Spread each slice of steak with mustard, sprinkle with chopped bacon and onion, parsley and pepper and top with a gherkin pickle or a piece of dill pickle. Roll up the beef slices and tie neatly with string.

In a shallow flameproof casserole or skillet, heat the oil and brown the beef rolls on all sides over brisk heat. Take them out, add the onion and cook gently until lightly browned.

Add the bouquet garni, wine, stock and seasoning, bring to a boil, replace the beef rolls, cover and simmer on top of the stove or braise in a moderately low oven (325°F) for $1\frac{1}{4}$–$1\frac{1}{2}$ hours or until the beef rolls are very tender.

Transfer the beef rolls to a platter and keep warm.

To make the sauce: in a saucepan melt the butter, stir in the flour and cook, stirring, until golden brown. Take from the heat, strain in the cooking liquid from the beef rolls and bring the sauce to a boil, stirring. Add the sour cream, bring almost back to a boil and taste for seasoning.

Spoon the sauce over the beef rolls and serve with braised red cabbage and potato dumplings (see page 127).

Braised Red Cabbage

1 medium head of red cabbage, shredded
2 tablespoons butter
1 onion, sliced
2 tart apples, pared, cored and sliced
2–3 tablespoons wine vinegar
$1\frac{1}{2}$ tablespoons sugar
salt and pepper
2–3 tablespoons water
kneaded butter, made with
  2 tablespoons butter and
  1 tablespoon flour

Braised cabbage is even better cooked the day before and reheated thoroughly just before serving.

Method
Blanch cabbage in a kettle of boiling water for 1 minute; drain. (The cabbage will turn deep violet at this point but when the vinegar is added it will return to its original color).

In a flameproof casserole melt the butter and fry the onion until soft but not brown. Add the apples, continue cooking 2–3 minutes and remove from the pan. Add cabbage in layers with the apple mixture, sprinkling the layers with vinegar, sugar, salt and pepper and water. Cover with buttered brown paper and the lid and braise in a moderately low oven (325°F) for $1\frac{1}{2}$–2 hours or until cabbage is very tender. Stir the cabbage occasionally and moisten with a little extra water if necessary.

Stir in the kneaded butter a little at a time, adding just enough to thicken the juices slightly. Adjust seasoning.

Rebhuhner in Sahne mit Weintrauben
(Partridge in Cream with Grapes)

4 partridges
1 tablespoon oil
4 slices of bacon, diced
1 onion, chopped
1 carrot, chopped
2 stalks of celery, chopped
1 apple, pared, cored and chopped
1 cup stock
1 cup white wine
2 tablespoons Schnaps or gin
1 cup sour cream
salt and pepper
$\frac{1}{4}$ teaspoon sugar
bunch of watercress (for garnish)

For stuffing
2 cups seedless green grapes, stems removed
4 tart apples, pared, cored and coarsely chopped
8 juniper berries, crushed
1–2 tablespoons sugar

Trussing needle and string

Squabs can be used instead of partridges for this recipe.

Method
To make the stuffing: mix the grapes, apples and crushed juniper berries and season with salt, pepper and sugar to taste. Fill the stuffing into the partridges and truss them.

In a flameproof casserole heat the oil and fry the bacon until it begins to brown. Drain and reserve it. Add the partridges and brown them on all sides. Take out, add the onion, carrot, celery and apple, lower the heat, cover the pot and cook 5–7 minutes or until the vegetables and apple are soft and the fat is absorbed.

Stir in the reserved bacon, place the partridges on top and pour in the stock and wine. Cover the pot, bring to a boil and braise in a moderately low oven (325°F) for 35–45 minutes or until the partridges are very tender.

Heat the Schnaps or gin, flame it and pour over the partridges. When the flame dies, set them on a platter and keep warm.

Work the sauce through a sieve so the vegetables are puréed — the mixture should be the consistency of heavy cream. Reheat the sauce, stir in the sour cream and heat gently.
Watchpoint: do not boil or it will curdle.

Add the salt, pepper and sugar to taste, spoon a little over the partridges and serve the rest separately.

Garnish the platter of partridges with a bunch of watercress and serve mashed potatoes as an accompaniment.

Schwäbisches Reh
(Swabian Roast Venison)

5–6 lb haunch or saddle of
   venison
$\frac{1}{4}$ lb piece of bacon, cut in
   1$\frac{1}{2}$ inch strips (for larding)
3 tablespoons meat drippings
   or lard
1 cup stock
1 cup sour cream

For marinade
2 cups red wine
2 cups water
2 tablespoons oil
1 onion, sliced
1 carrot, sliced
bouquet garni
5 juniper berries, crushed
6 peppercorns

For garnish
1 can (14 oz) chanterelle
   (Pfifferlinge) mushrooms
1 cup ($\frac{1}{4}$ lb) button mushrooms
3 tablespoons butter
1 tablespoon chopped parsley
salt and pepper
3 cups cranberry sauce

Larding needle

Method
Lard the venison with the
bacon strips (see page 129).

In a saucepan bring all the
ingredients for the marinade
to a boil and simmer 5 minutes; let cool.

Set the venison in a deep
bowl (not aluminum) and pour
over the marinade – it should
cover the meat. Cover and
refrigerate for 3–6 days – the
older the animal and the
stronger you like the flavor
of the meat, the longer the
venison should marinate.

Drain the venison and pat
dry with paper towels; strain
and reserve the marinade.

In a roasting pan heat the
meat drippings or lard, put in

the venison and baste with
hot fat. Add 1 cup of strained
marinade and stock; roast in
moderately hot oven (375°F)
for 1$\frac{1}{4}$-1$\frac{1}{2}$ hours for rare meat
or 1$\frac{3}{4}$-2 hours for well done
meat, basting often and add-
ing more marinade if the pan
gets dry.

To make the garnish: drain
the chanterelle mushrooms
thoroughly and trim the button mushroom stems level
with the caps. In a pan heat
the butter, add the button
mushrooms and sauté 2–3
minutes or until tender. Add
the chanterelle mushrooms,
cook 1–2 minutes until very
hot and add the chopped
parsley with seasoning; keep
warm.

Transfer the venison to a

platter and keep warm. Skim
any fat from the roasting pan,
add the remaining marinade
and the stock and boil until
reduced to about 1$\frac{1}{2}$ cups.
Stir in the sour cream, heat
gently without boiling and
taste for seasoning.

Garnish the venison with
the mushrooms, and serve the
cranberry sauce and sour
cream sauce separately.
Spätzle are a good accom-
paniment (see recipe on page
129).

*Schwäbisches Reh (roast leg
of venison) is accompanied
by button and chanterelle
mushrooms, buttered Spätzle,
cranberry sauce and a rich
sour cream sauce*

Many types of **mush-
rooms** grow wild in
Germany, including Pfif-
ferlinge (chanterelle), a
golden-yellow fluted cup
with a slightly spicy flavor.

Speisemorcheln (mor-
els) are pitted and dark
and are particularly valued
for their rich flavor;
Waldegerlinge are field
mushrooms that have a
more musky flavor than
their cultivated cousins,
button mushrooms.

Chanterelles are avail-
able dried or in cans;
morels are available
dried.

Cranberry Sauce

4 cups (1 lb) fresh cranberries
1 cup sugar (or to taste)
1 cup water
1 tablespoon port (optional)

Makes about 3 cups.

Method
Wash and pick over the fresh
cranberries.

Dissolve the sugar in the
water, bring to a boil and
simmer 2 minutes over low
heat. Add the cranberries and
simmer, uncovered, for 5
minutes or until the cranberries are just tender. Take
them from the heat and add
the port, if used, and more
sugar to taste.

If you prefer a pulpy sauce,
cook the cranberries 1–2 minutes longer, then crush them
lightly with a wooden spoon
to break them up.

Cover the cranberry sauce
and let stand in the refrigerator until needed.

Marianne's Streusel Kuchen

For dough
about 1 cup lukewarm milk
$3\frac{1}{2}$ cups flour
$\frac{1}{4}$ cup sugar
1 cake compressed yeast or
   1 package dry yeast
$\frac{1}{2}$ teaspoon salt
1 egg

For topping
1 cup butter
$1\frac{3}{4}$ cups flour
1 cup sugar
1 teaspoon ground cinnamon
juice of $\frac{1}{2}$ lemon

Method
To make the dough: in a cup measure stir 2 tablespoons of the milk into 1 teaspoon of the flour and 1 teaspoon of the sugar. Sprinkle or crumble the yeast on top and stir to mix. Let stand in a warm place for 15–20 minutes or until the mixture froths to the top of the measure.

Sift the remaining flour and the salt into a bowl and sprinkle the remaining sugar on top. Make a well in the center, add the yeast mixture, egg and the remaining milk. Mix with the hand to a smooth dough, adding more milk if necessary to make a soft but slightly sticky dough.

Turn the dough out onto a lightly floured board and knead 5 minutes or until the dough is smooth and elastic. Transfer it to a floured bowl, cover with a damp cloth and let rise in a warm place for $1\frac{1}{2}$ hours or until it is doubled in bulk.

To make the topping: cream the butter, add the flour, sugar and cinnamon and work with the fingertips until the mixture forms large crumbs. Sprinkle over the lemon juice, work the topping lightly until mixed, then chill it.

Set the oven at moderate (350°F).

Knead the dough lightly to knock out the air, transfer it to a greased baking sheet and pat it out, oiling your hand so it does not stick, to a 9 X 12 inch rectangle about $\frac{1}{2}$ inch thick.

Spread over the topping so the dough cannot be seen. Let rise in a warm place for 30–40 minutes or until it is almost doubled in bulk. Bake in the heated oven for 15 minutes or until the topping is browned. Transfer to a wire rack to cool and cut in squares to serve.

Frucht Streusel Kuchen

Follow the recipe for Marianne's Streusel Kuchen but make only half the topping.

Pat out the dough on a greased baking sheet and cover it with 5–6 tart apples, pared, cored, thinly sliced and arranged in overlapping slices, or with 2 lb fresh prune plums, halved and pitted.

Sprinkle the dough with topping, let rise and bake as for Marianne's Streusel Kuchen, for 25–30 minutes or until the fruit is tender.

Haselnusskuchen (Hazelnut Coffeecake)

$\frac{3}{4}$ cup shelled hazelnuts, browned and chopped (see box)
3 cups flour
1 package dry or 1 cake compressed yeast
1 cup lukewarm milk
3 eggs, beaten to mix
$\frac{1}{2}$ cup butter
$\frac{1}{4}$ cup sugar
pinch of salt
$\frac{3}{4}$ cup raisins
$\frac{3}{4}$ cup apricot jam glaze, melted with 1 teaspoon dry instant coffee, or soft icing made with $\frac{1}{2}$ cup sifted confectioners' sugar mixed with $1\frac{1}{2}$ teaspoons water

For honey nut coating
6 tablespoons thick honey
$\frac{1}{2}$ cup slivered or shredded almonds
$\frac{3}{4}$ cup shelled hazelnuts, browned and chopped
$\frac{1}{2}$ cup butter
$\frac{1}{4}$ cup sugar
$\frac{1}{2}$ cup flour

7–8 inch kugelhopf or tube pan

Method
To make the dough: sift the flour into a warm bowl and make a well in the center. Sprinkle or crumble the yeast over the lukewarm milk, let stand 5 minutes until dissolved, then add to the flour with the beaten eggs.

Work in the flour to form a smooth dough and beat 5 minutes with your hand until the dough is very smooth and elastic. Cover the bowl with a damp cloth and let rise in a warm place for 40–50 minutes or until the dough is doubled in bulk.

To make the honey nut coating: cream the butter, beat in the sugar until soft and light, then beat in the honey and flour to make a smooth paste. Stir in the almonds and $\frac{3}{4}$ cup hazelnuts. Spread the mixture evenly over the surface of the pan and chill.

When the dough has risen, work it lightly to knock out the air. Cream the $\frac{1}{2}$ cup butter and beat it into the dough with the sugar and salt, then work in the raisins and remaining $\frac{3}{4}$ cup hazelnuts.

Transfer the dough to the prepared pan, cover and let stand in a warm place for 45–55 minutes or until the dough rises to the top of the pan. Set the oven at hot (400°F).

Bake the kuchen in the heated oven for 45 minutes or until well browned and a skewer inserted near the center comes out clean. Turn out onto a wire rack to cool.

When cold, brush with the melted apricot jam glaze and coffee mixture to darken the surface of the finished kuchen or with the soft confectioners' sugar icing.

To brown hazelnuts: bake them in a moderately hot oven (375°F) for 8–10 minutes. Then rub them briskly in a rough cloth to remove the dry skins. Grind the nuts in a rotary cheese grater or work a few at a time in a blender.

Haselnusskuchen, made with hazelnuts, is one of many popular German yeast breads

Apfeltorte
(Meringue Apple Cake)

5–6 tart apples, pared, cored and sliced
¼ cup raisins
2 tablespoons mixed chopped candied peel
2 tablespoons sugar (or to taste)
¼ cup slivered almonds, chopped (for decoration)

For pastry
2 cups flour
1 teaspoon baking powder
pinch of salt
½ teaspoon ground cinnamon
½ cup butter
½ cup sugar
1 egg yolk, beaten
3 tablespoons ice water

For icing
½ cup sugar
2 tablespoons flour
pinch of salt
1½ cups milk
1 egg, beaten to mix
1 teaspoon rum

For meringue
2 egg whites
½ cup sugar
½ teaspoon vanilla

9 inch springform pan; pastry bag and medium star tube

Method
To make the pastry dough: sift the flour into a bowl with the baking powder, salt and cinnamon. Cut in the butter, then rub with the fingertips until the mixture resembles crumbs. Add the sugar, then stir in the beaten egg to form a dough; work lightly with the hand, gradually adding enough ice water to make a smooth dough. Chill 30 minutes.

Set oven at moderately hot (375°F).

Roll out the dough and line the springform pan, bring-ing the pastry 1 inch up the sides of the pan. Fill the pastry shell with half the apples, sprinkle with the raisins, candied peel and sugar to taste and add remaining apples. Bake in the heated oven for 45 minutes or until the apples are just tender and the pastry is browned. Let the cake cool and remove the sides of the pan.

To make the icing: in a heavy based pan, combine the sugar, flour and salt. Stir in the milk and heat the mixture, stirring constantly, until it thickens. Take from the heat, beat in the egg and cook again, stirring until the icing thickens slightly. At once take it from the heat and stir in the rum. Let cool to lukewarm and pour it over the top of the cake to coat it.

To make the meringue: stiffly whip the egg whites. Add 1 tablespoon sugar and continue beating until the mixture is glossy. Fold in the remaining sugar with the vanilla.

Put the meringue in a pastry bag fitted with a star tube and pipe rosettes around the edge of the cake. Sprinkle each rosette with chopped almonds and bake in the heated oven for 8–10 minutes or until the meringue is browned. Let the cake cool and leave on the springform pan base to serve.

Mouth-watering Apfeltorte is an apple and raisin filled pastry shell, topped with icing and meringue, and sprinkled with almonds before browning

The Christmas season is celebrated in a platter of anise- and lemon-flavored picture cookies called Springerle. Wooden molds shown are a roller of 12 patterns, an individual mold and a block of 6 patterns

Springerle
(Molded Christmas Cookies)

$\frac{1}{2}-\frac{3}{4}$ cup aniseed
4 eggs
2 cups sugar
grated rind of 1 lemon
1 tablespoon brandy
4 cups flour

Springerle mold

Makes 24—26 cookies each 2 X $3\frac{1}{2}$ inches.

Method
Grease 2 baking sheets and sprinkle them generously with aniseed.

Beat the eggs until mixed, gradually beat in the sugar and continue beating for 15 minutes or until the mixture is thick and light and leaves a ribbon trail when the whisk or beater is lifted. Beat in the lemon rind and brandy.

Sift the flour and stir it into the egg mixture, then work with the hand, adding a little more flour if necessary to make a dough that is smooth but not sticky. Knead it on a floured board for 10 minutes until satiny, working in more flour if the dough starts to stick. Cover and let stand 1 hour.

Roll out the dough to $\frac{3}{8}$ inch thickness and cut into pieces the size of the mold. Sprinkle the mold with flour and tap it on the table to remove excess flour. Press the pieces of dough firmly into the mold or roll them on the mold with a rolling pin so the design is clearly impressed.

Lay the dough, design side up, on the prepared baking sheets and let dry, uncovered, for 24 hours.

Set the oven at low (250°F). Bake the cookies in the heated oven for 20—25 min-
utes or until firm. The tops should be white and the bottoms lightly browned. Transfer the cookies to a wire rack to cool, then cover them and leave in a cool airy place for 1—2 weeks to soften and mellow.

Springerle molds are made of wood in a wide variety of sizes and designs. They are available in many cooking equipment stores and make attractive as well as practical kitchen decorations.

Pfeffernüsse
(German 'Peppery Nuts')

1 cup sugar
2 eggs, separated
2 cups flour
$1\frac{1}{2}$ teaspoons ground cinnamon
$\frac{1}{4}$ teaspoon ground ginger
$\frac{1}{4}$ teaspoon ground cardamom
$\frac{1}{4}$ teaspoon ground allspice
$\frac{1}{4}$ teaspoon ground white pepper
3 tablespoons finely chopped candied citron
grated rind of 1 lemon
2—3 tablespoons whole almonds, blanched and ground

To finish
3—4 tablespoons rum
confectioners' sugar (for rolling)
candied cherries, cut in pieces

Makes 33—36 pfeffernüsse.

Method
Beat half the sugar with egg yolks until mixture is light and fluffy. Sift flour with all the spices and stir into egg yolk mixture. Whip egg whites until they hold a stiff peak and beat in remaining sugar until glossy. Stir gently into flour mixture with citron, lemon rind and almonds. Cover bowl and let stand in refrigerator overnight.

Set oven at moderately hot (375°F) and butter a baking sheet. Roll and press the rather crumbly mixture into walnut-sized balls, set on baking sheet and bake in heated oven 18—20 minutes or until lightly browned. Sprinkle them with rum while warm and roll in confectioners' sugar.

Store in an airtight container for at least a week to mellow — pfeffernüsse will keep well for several weeks. Just before serving, roll again in confectioners' sugar and top with a piece of candied cherry.

Waldmeister- bowle
(Woodruff or May Wine)

2 large bunches of fresh woodruff or 1 cup dried woodruff
$\frac{1}{2}$ cup superfine (or bar) sugar
2 bottles of sparkling Moselle wine
1 quart fresh strawberries (optional)

This wine cup is traditionally made in May, when fresh woodruff is at its best before it comes into flower. The herb gives a pleasantly aromatic flavor to the wine.

Method
Tie the woodruff with string, place it in a punch bowl and sprinkle over the sugar. Pour over 1 bottle of the wine, cover and stand for $\frac{1}{2}$—1 hour or until the wine is flavored to your taste.

Lift out the fresh woodruff or remove the dried woodruff with a slotted spoon. Add the strawberries, if using, and chill thoroughly. Just before serving, add the remaining bottle of wine.

INDEX

(Volume 11)

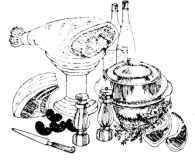

M

N

OP

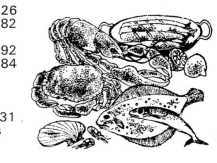

Q

R

S

Acknowledgments
Photographs by Fred J. Maroon on pages 16, 18, 30, 38, 80, 83, 85, 88, 90, 94 and 107. Photographs by Ross Chapple on pages 122, 126, 130, 132, 134, 135 and 136; styling by Fay Abell. Photograph on page 50 courtesy of Cannon's Seafood, Washington D.C. Other photographs by Michael Leale, John Ledger, John Cowderoy and Michael Davies. Fish information courtesy of National Fisheries Council. Accessories – pages 122 and 132: tapestry from Peter Mack Brown Antiques, Washington D.C.; pages 126 and 128: tableware from The China Closet, Washington D.C.; page 135: rolling pin mold from The German Delicatessen, Washington D.C.; individual angel mold from Iberian Imports, Alexandria, Virginia; block mold and cookie platter from The China Closet, Washington D.C.